ANCIENT GREECE

Bronze mirror cover
showing Aphrodite
playing knucklebones
with Pan, 350 B.C.

Round-
mouthed
jug with
coins

Griffin's-
head *rhyton*

Bronze banqueter
figurine

Aphrodite
removing her
sandal

Theseus
and the
Minotaur

Kylix

Bronze
chariot
fitting

EYEWITNESS BOOKS

ANCIENT GREECE

Written by
ANNE PEARSON

Stoddart

Wine
strainer

Oil container

Bronze cymbals

DK

A DORLING KINDERSLEY BOOK

Project editor Gillian Denton
Art editor Liz Sephton
Managing editor Helen Parker
Managing art editor Julia Harris
Production Louise Barratt
Picture research Diana Morris
Special photography Nick Nicholls
Additional photography Liz McAulay

This Eyewitness ™ Guide has been conceived by
Dorling Kindersley Limited and Editions Gallimard

First published in Canada in 1992 by
Stoddart Publishing Co. Limited
34 Lesmill Road, Toronto, Canada M3B 2T6

First published in Great Britain in 1992 by
Dorling Kindersley Limited, London
9 Henrietta Street, London WC2E 8PS

Reprinted in 1995

Copyright © Dorling Kindersley Limited, London 1992

Canadian Cataloguing in Publication Data

Pearson, Anne.
Ancient Greece

(Eyewitness books)
ISBN 0-7737-2608-X

1. Greece - Civilization - To 146 B.C. - Juvenile
literature. 2. Greece - History - To 146 B.C. -
Juvenile literature. I. title. II. Series

DF77. P43 1992   j938   C92-093689-X
Color reproduction by Colourscan, Singapore
Printed in Singapore by Toppan

Terra-cotta
dancing woman

Terra-cotta
figurine of a
youth with hat

Griffin earrings

Rattle shaped like a pig

Contents

Child's toy

The Greek world

THE BRITISH MUSEUM
The architecture of the British Museum in London was inspired by Classical Greek architecture. The first part of the museum was completed in 1827 and the building as it is today gradually arose over the next 30 years. Many of the objects in this book can be seen there.

T HE LAND OF GREECE is made up of mainland Greece and numerous islands scattered throughout the Aegean and Adriatic seas. It is a mountainous country with hot, dry summers and rain only in winter. The early Greek settlements developed as small independent communities cut off from each other by the mountains and often competing for the best land, because fertile soil is in short supply. Each of the "city-states" that developed out of these communities had a strong individual identity, and citizens were loyal to their home state and its patron deity (god). This miscellaneous collection of city-states sometimes joined together for mutual defense, most successfully against the Persians in the 490s and 480s B.C. The Greeks produced a glorious culture, which has had a profound effect on Western civilization through succeeding centuries, right down to the present day. The ancient Greeks scaled the heights in literature, visual and dramatic arts, philosophy, politics, sports, and many other aspects of human life. Greek civilization reached its peak in Athens in the fifth century B.C.

KOUROS
Kouroi (marble statues of naked boys) were made mainly in the sixth century B.C. to decorate sanctuaries of the gods, particularly Apollo, but some may have been put up in memory of young soldiers who had died in battle. They stand with their arms by their sides and one foot in front of the other.

THE ANCIENT GREEK WORLD
This map shows ancient Greece and the surrounding area. It includes towns established by the first emigrants from the mainland who traveled east. The emigrants settled on Ionia, a coastal area of Asia Minor. The names of the regions are in capitals and the cities are in small letters.

THRACE

MACEDON

Troy

AEGEAN SEA

Pergamum

LYDIA

Delphi

Smyrna

IONIA

Plataea
Thebes
Eleusis
Athens

Ephesus

IONIAN SEA

Corinth
Tiryns
Olympia
Mycenae

Miletus

Didyma
Halicarnassus

CARIA

Theangela

N

Sparta

LYCIA

Phylakopi

Akrotiri

Camirus

Knossos
Mallia
CRETE

Phaistos
Zakro

SCALE
Km
150
Miles
100

ACROPOLIS
Athens (pp. 16–17) was the most important city of ancient Greece, and the center for all forms of arts and learning. Its Acropolis (fortified hill) was crowned with the temple of the Parthenon, dedicated to the goddess Athena.

DONKEY DRINKING CUP
Beautifully painted pottery was a specialty of the Greeks. It was used mainly for storing, mixing, serving, and drinking wine. This is a special two-handled cup in the form of a donkey's head.

HIPPOCAMP
The gold ring is decorated with a hippocamp, a sea horse with two forefeet and a body ending in the tail of a dolphin or a fish.

GREECE AND THE WIDER WORLD
This chart shows the rise and fall of the Greek world from Minoan times (pp. 8–9) to the end of the Hellenistic period. These historic events can be seen against a background of other civilizations in Europe, Asia, and South America.

DATES B.C.	2000–1500	1500–1100	1100–800	800–480	480–323	323–30
EVENTS IN GREECE	Cretan palace (Minoan) civilization.	Fall of Knossos. Rise and fall of Mycenaean civilization.	The foundation of Sparta. The formation of Homeric poems.	Ionian and Black Sea colonies founded. First Olympic Games.	Persian invasions. Start of democracy in Athens. Sparta controls the Peloponnesus. Age of Pericles.	Rise of Macedon. Fall of Sparta. Life of Alexander. Wars of Alexander's successors.
CULTURAL PERIOD	Bronze Age	Bronze Age	Dark Age	Archaic Age	Classical Age	Hellenistic Age
WORLD EVENTS	Indus Valley civilizations in India.	Hittite Empire in Asia. Babylonian Empire. Mayan civilization in Central America. Chang dynasty in China.	Celtic peoples arrive in Britain. Phoenician colonies in Spain. Olmec civilization in Mexico.	Rise of Etruscans in Italy. Kushites invade Egypt. Rome founded. Assyrian Empire.	Confucius born in China. Assyrians conquer lower Egypt. Persian Empire.	Toltecs settle in central Mexico. Ch'in dynasty in China. Great Wall built in China.

MARATHON MEN
Athletics was a favorite pastime in ancient Greece (pp. 44–45). Games took place as part of religious festivals. These three runners are painted on a pot that was given as a prize to the winner of the race at the Panathenaic Games held in Athens in honor of Athena (pp. 16–17).

GOD SCENT
Greece was much influenced by the East. This little *aryballos* (perfume pot) of a baboon was made by a craftsman at Naucratis, a Greek trading town in the Nile Delta in Egypt. In Egyptian mythology, Thoth, the god of wisdom, was represented as a baboon.

DECORATING WITH DOLPHINS
The walls of the Minoan palaces were richly decorated with painted scenes known as frescoes, made by applying paint to wet plaster. Many we see today are modern reconstructions based on fragments of painted plaster that have survived. This famous dolphin fresco is from the queen's apartment at Knossos.

Minoan civilization

THE FIRST GREAT CIVILIZATION of the Aegean world flourished on the island of Crete. The area was inhabited as early as 6000 B.C., and the island reached the height of its power between 2200 B.C. and 1450 B.C. Its wealth was a result of its thriving trade with other Bronze Age towns in Greece, the Mediterranean, Egypt, and Syria. Prosperity also came from the rich Cretan soil, which produced oil, grain, and wine grapes in abundance. The economy was based around rich palaces, the remains of which have been found in different parts of the island. This peaceful Cretan civilization is known as Minoan, after a legendary king of Crete called Minos. Knossos and the other palaces were destroyed by fire around 1700 B.C., after which they were rebuilt, even more luxuriously. From then until about 1500 B.C., Minoan civilization was at its height.

WORSHIPER
This bronze figure is in an attitude of worship of the gods.

CRETE
This map shows the main towns and palaces on Crete, at Knossos, Zakro, Phaistos, and Mallia. A large villa has also been found at Hagia Triada. Most of the settlements were built close to the sea. The remains of the lavish buildings are evidence of the skill of Minoan architects, engineers, and artists. Not everyone lived in the palaces. Some lived in smaller town houses or in farmhouses in the country. It is said that the young Zeus was brought up in the Dictaean Cave on the high plain of Lassithi.

TAKING THE BULL BY THE HORNS
The bull was regarded by the Minoans as a sacred animal. A Greek myth tells the story of the god Zeus falling in love with a beautiful princess called Europa. Zeus turned himself into a white bull and swam to Crete with Europa on his back. They had three sons, one of whom was Minos, who became the king of Crete. Daring bull sports became a way of worshiping the bull. This bronze figure shows a boy somersaulting over a bull's horns.

BULL MURAL
This mural at Knossos shows an acrobat leaping over a bull.

DISCOVERING KNOSSOS
English archeologist Sir Arthur Evans discovered the largest of the Minoan palaces at Knossos in 1894. He dug there for several years, and the remains of the colossal building he found, with its hundreds of rooms, amazed the world.

THESEUS AND THE MINOTAUR
According to Greek legend a young prince of Athens called Theseus went to Crete and killed a monster, half-man, half-bull to whom Athenian children were sent as a sacrifice every year.. The monster, the Minotaur, was kept in a maze called the Labyrinth. The huge palace at Knossos has many long, winding corridors; it may have been modeled after the Labyrinth.

MODERN MINOTAUR
The story of the conflict between Theseus and the Minotaur was popular not only with Greek vase painters but also with many modern artists. The interpretation above by Spanish artist Pablo Picasso (1881-1973) is almost as difficult to unravel as the maze!

RESTORATION AND RECONSTRUCTION
The palace of Knossos was made of stone with wooden roofs and ceilings. It was built and rebuilt several times, and some parts of it were four stories high. It had royal apartments, including a throne room where the ruler of Knossos would sit in splendor. Sir Arthur Evans restored some of the palace, so it is now possible to get a sense of what it was like when it was new. The wooden columns are painted the same shade of red as the original stories.

The Mycenaean civilization

GREECE IN THE BRONZE AGE (before iron tools and weapons came into use) had several important centers, including Mycenae. Mycenae, city of the legendary king Agamemnon, was one of several heavily fortified strongholds. The king or chief lived in a palace with many rooms that served as a military headquarters and administrative center for the surrounding countryside. The Mycenaeans were warriors, and weapons and armor have been found in their graves. They were also great traders and sailed far and wide. Their civilization reached its height of power about 1600 B.C. and eclipsed the Minoan civilization of Crete. All seemed secure and prosperous, but around 1250 B.C. the Mycenaeans came under threat from foreign invaders and started to build huge defensive walls around all the major towns. By about 1200 B.C. the cities began to be abandoned or destroyed. Within 100 years the Mycenaean strongholds had fallen and a period often called the Dark Ages had begun.

POMEGRANATE PENDANT
This little gold pendant in the form of a pomegranate was found on the island of Cyprus. It was made by a Mycenaean craftsman around 1300 B.C. and is a good example of a jewelry technique called granulation. Tiny gold granules grouped in triangles decorate its surface. Mycenaean artists and traders settled in Cyprus in large numbers. The island later provided a refuge for many Greeks fleeing from unrest at home as the Mycenaean civilization crumbled.

BULL SPRINKLER
This clay bull's head was used as a ritual sprinkler at religious ceremonies. There are small holes in the mouth to let the water escape. These sprinklers are sometimes in the shape of other animals, but bulls are the most common.

OCTOPUS JAR
This pottery jar with a painting of an octopus was found in a cemetery at a Mycenaean colony on the island of Rhodes. Mycenaean artists were much influenced by Minoan work, and subjects like this, inspired by the sea, continued to be popular.

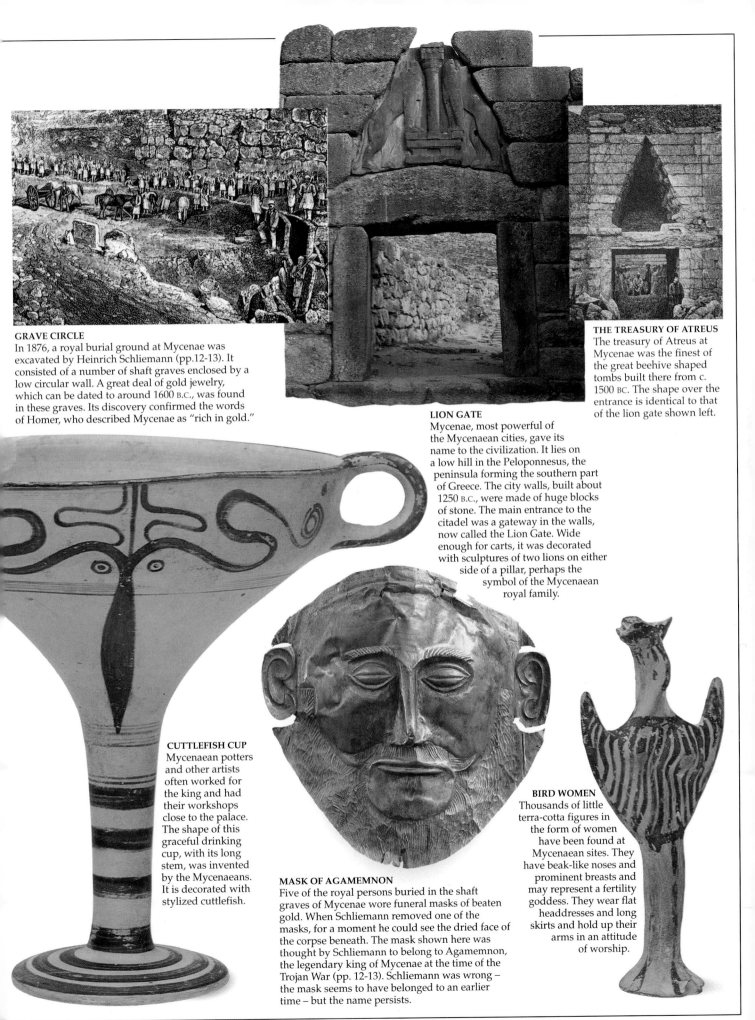

GRAVE CIRCLE
In 1876, a royal burial ground at Mycenae was excavated by Heinrich Schliemann (pp.12-13). It consisted of a number of shaft graves enclosed by a low circular wall. A great deal of gold jewelry, which can be dated to around 1600 B.C., was found in these graves. Its discovery confirmed the words of Homer, who described Mycenae as "rich in gold."

THE TREASURY OF ATREUS
The treasury of Atreus at Mycenae was the finest of the great beehive shaped tombs built there from c. 1500 BC. The shape over the entrance is identical to that of the lion gate shown left.

LION GATE
Mycenae, most powerful of the Mycenaean cities, gave its name to the civilization. It lies on a low hill in the Peloponnesus, the peninsula forming the southern part of Greece. The city walls, built about 1250 B.C., were made of huge blocks of stone. The main entrance to the citadel was a gateway in the walls, now called the Lion Gate. Wide enough for carts, it was decorated with sculptures of two lions on either side of a pillar, perhaps the symbol of the Mycenaean royal family.

CUTTLEFISH CUP
Mycenaean potters and other artists often worked for the king and had their workshops close to the palace. The shape of this graceful drinking cup, with its long stem, was invented by the Mycenaeans. It is decorated with stylized cuttlefish.

MASK OF AGAMEMNON
Five of the royal persons buried in the shaft graves of Mycenae wore funeral masks of beaten gold. When Schliemann removed one of the masks, for a moment he could see the dried face of the corpse beneath. The mask shown here was thought by Schliemann to belong to Agamemnon, the legendary king of Mycenae at the time of the Trojan War (pp. 12-13). Schliemann was wrong – the mask seems to have belonged to an earlier time – but the name persists.

BIRD WOMEN
Thousands of little terra-cotta figures in the form of women have been found at Mycenaean sites. They have beak-like noses and prominent breasts and may represent a fertility goddess. They wear flat headdresses and long skirts and hold up their arms in an attitude of worship.

To Troy and back

IN THE 12TH CENTURY B.C., the rich Mycenaean towns and palaces fell into decline or were destroyed, trade with the East decreased, and Greece entered a dark age. During the next few centuries, stories of the great Mycenaean civilization that had gone before were handed down from one generation to the next in the form of poems. Two of them, *The Iliad* and *The Odyssey,* have survived. They reached their final form in the eighth century B.C. at the hands of the poet Homer, whose poetry was admired throughout the Greek world. *The Iliad* describes how a city called Troy, on the west coast of modern Turkey, was besieged by a Greek army led by King Agamemnon of Mycenae. It describes the heroic deeds of Greek and Trojan soldiers like Achilles and Hektor. *The Odyssey* tells the story of the return home from the Trojan War of one Greek hero, Odysseus. It took him ten years and he had many adventures along the way. The Homeric stories reflect real incidents of wars, battles, and sieges from an earlier age. It is probable that war was waged between the Greeks and the Trojans, possibly over the ownership of lands and crops at a time when the Mycenaean world was falling apart, and not over the recapture of Helen (above).

HELEN OF TROY
Helen was the beautiful wife of Menelaus, king of Sparta and brother of Agamemnon, king of Mycenae. According to legend, Helen's capture by Paris, son of Priam, who was king of Troy, caused the Trojan War. The Greeks united to defeat the Trojans and restore Helen to her husband.

HEINRICH SCHLIEMANN
In 1870, German archaeologist Heinrich Schliemann (1822–1890) discovered the site of ancient Troy near the Mediterranean coast in modern Turkey. He had been looking for it for many years. His excavations revealed not just one city, but more than nine of them, built on top of each other. (It is not certain which layer is the city described in *The Iliad*.) Frau Schliemann is wearing some of the superb jewelry found at Troy.

MODERN MODEL
In Troy today, there is a modern replica of the Trojan horse. It is very large and, like the ancient one, is made of wood. Children can climb a ladder into its stomach and pretend to be Greek soldiers.

OVERCOME BY CURIOSITY
Troy withstood the Greeks' siege for ten long years. In the end, the Greeks triumphed by a trick. They constructed a huge wooden horse, which they left just outside the city. The Trojans then watched the Greek army sail away and, overcome with curiosity, dragged the horse inside the city walls. Late that night, Greek soldiers, hidden inside the horse, crept out and opened the city gates. The Greek army, which had silently returned, entered and destroyed the city. This picture of the horse comes from a pot of about 650–600 B.C.

THE WOODEN HORSE
The story of Troy and the wooden horse has been a favorite with artists through the centuries. Italian artist Giovanni Tiepolo (1696–1770) painted more than one version of the subject.

THE BLINDING OF POLYPHEMUS

In one of his adventures on his way home from the Trojan War, the hero Odysseus met a Cyclops called Polyphemus, a man-eating giant with only one eye, in the middle of his forehead. Odysseus and his men were trapped in Polyphemus' cave and the giant started to eat them one by one. Cunning Odysseus brought the giant a skin full of wine, which lulled him into a drunken sleep. Then he blinded Polyphemus by driving a red-hot stake into his only eye.

PATIENT PENELOPE

After his ten-year journey, Odysseus returned at last to Ithaca, his island home, and to his wife, Penelope. During his long absence, she had waited patiently for him, even though everyone else had given him up for dead. When other men proposed marriage to Penelope, she told them that she would give them an answer when she had finished weaving a particular piece of cloth. At night, Penelope crept secretly to her loom and undid everything she had woven during the day. In this way, she postponed indefinitely her reply to her suitors. In this painting by British artist John Stanhope (1829–1908), Penelope is sitting sadly beside her loom.

WOOLLY ESCAPE

Polyphemus kept a flock of sheep in the cave at night and these provided a means of escape. Odysseus and his men tied themselves underneath the sheep. In the morning, the flock filed out of the cave to graze. The blind giant felt the backs of the sheep in case his captives were hiding there, but he did not think to feel under their bellies. This story has been illustrated on a black-figure vase (pp. 48-49).

Blue paint indicating sea

Helmet

MOTHER TO THE RESCUE

The mother of Achilles was a sea nymph called Thetis. This little terra-cotta figurine shows Thetis or one of her sisters riding the waves on a sea horse, bringing a new helmet for Achilles to wear in battle. Some of the bright blue paint, representing the sea, still survives.

DEATH OF A HERO

After the Greek champion Achilles had killed the bravest Trojan warrior, Hektor, he tied Hektor's body to a chariot and dragged it three times around the walls of Troy. On this clay lamp, Achilles can be seen driving the chariot and looking back in triumph. Above him, on the walls of Troy, Hektor's parents, King Priam and Queen Hecuba, watch in horror.

Greek expansion

GREECE STARTED TO EMERGE from the Dark Ages in the eighth century B.C. Trading posts began to be established abroad, as far away as the Nile Delta in Egypt. As the population expanded and Greek agriculture could no longer meet the needs of the people, some towns sent out colonies both east- and westward. They settled in southern Italy, Sicily, and other parts of the western Mediterranean, and in the East around the shores of the Black Sea. Some of these colonies were very rich. It was said that the people of Sybaris in southern Italy slept on beds of rose petals, and roosters were banned from the town so that the inhabitants would not be woken too early in the morning. Greek culture was influenced by foreign styles. The Geometric style, which, as its name suggests, was dominated by geometric patterns, gave way to a new, so-called Orientalizing style. Designs influenced by the East, such as griffins and sphinxes, were introduced. Egypt and Syria were the main sources. Corinth, Rhodes, and Ephesus were well placed for Eastern trade and became rich.

GOLDEN GRIFFINS
These gold griffin heads, inspired by the East, were found on the island of Rhodes. They were made in the seventh century B.C. and were once attached to a pair of earrings.

MAN SIZE
The Greeks liked to wear bangles decorated with animal heads. This lion-headed bangle, which is silver-plated, may have been worn by a man.

FOND FAREWELL
This detail is from a large pot decorated in the Geometric style. The rigid figures are painted in silhouette. The man on the right is leaving the woman and stepping onto a boat. Perhaps he is meant to be the hero Odysseus saying goodbye to his wife, Penelope, before he goes off to the Trojan War (pp. 12–13), or possibly he is Paris abducting Helen.

FAIENCE FROG
At this time in Greek history, there was much interest in Egyptian art, and the craftsman who made this may have been copying Egyptian work. It shows a man kneeling and holding a jar on top of which is a frog, a sacred creature in Egyptian religion. The object is made of faience, a greenish material often used to make Egyptian ornaments.

LION *ARYBALLOS*
This *aryballos* (perfume pot), which probably came from Thebes, has a spout in the shape of a lion's head. In spite of its small size, it has three zones of painted figures upon it. A horse race can be seen, along with warriors walking in procession. At the bottom is a tiny scene of dogs chasing hares. The mouth of this pot would have been filled with wax to prevent the evaporation of the perfume inside.

EXOTIC EXPORTS
Many little perfume pots were made in the town of Corinth and exported all over the Greek world. They are often in curious shapes and prettily decorated. The winged figure painted on this one may represent a god of the wind.

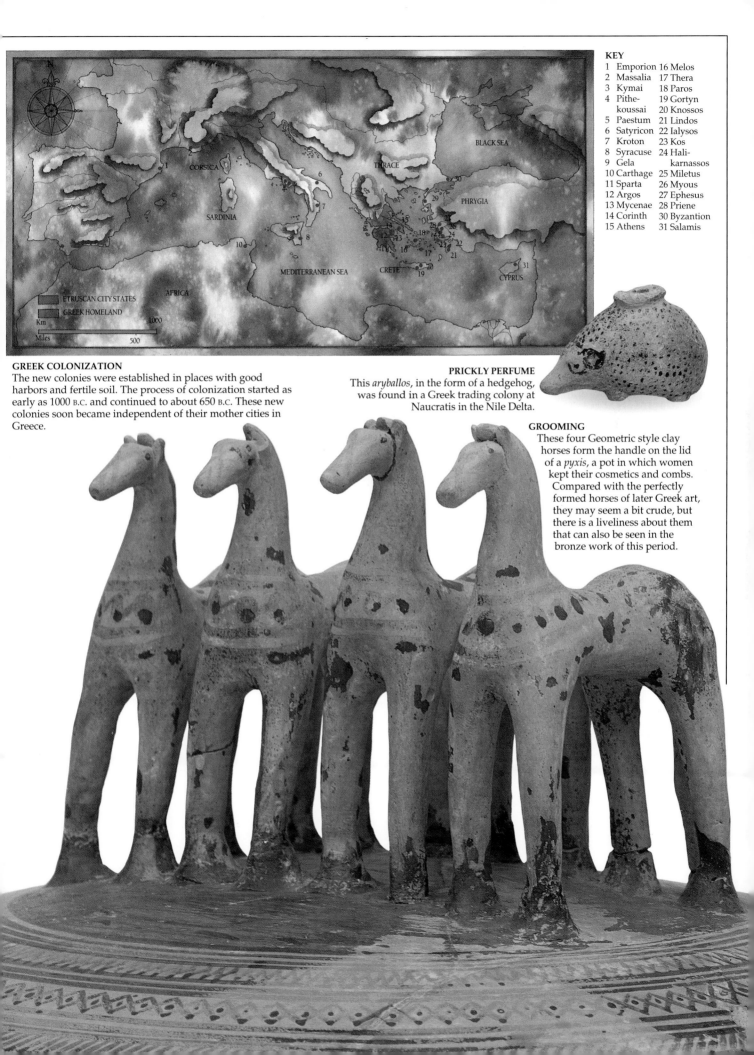

KEY

1 Emporion	16 Melos
2 Massalia	17 Thera
3 Kymai	18 Paros
4 Pithe-	19 Gortyn
koussai	20 Knossos
5 Paestum	21 Lindos
6 Satyricon	22 Ialysos
7 Kroton	23 Kos
8 Syracuse	24 Hali-
9 Gela	karnassos
10 Carthage	25 Miletus
11 Sparta	26 Myous
12 Argos	27 Ephesus
13 Mycenae	28 Priene
14 Corinth	30 Byzantion
15 Athens	31 Salamis

GREEK COLONIZATION

The new colonies were established in places with good harbors and fertile soil. The process of colonization started as early as 1000 B.C. and continued to about 650 B.C. These new colonies soon became independent of their mother cities in Greece.

PRICKLY PERFUME

This *aryballos*, in the form of a hedgehog, was found in a Greek trading colony at Naucratis in the Nile Delta.

GROOMING

These four Geometric style clay horses form the handle on the lid of a *pyxis*, a pot in which women kept their cosmetics and combs. Compared with the perfectly formed horses of later Greek art, they may seem a bit crude, but there is a liveliness about them that can also be seen in the bronze work of this period.

Athens, city of Athena

ATHENS WAS THE MOST POWERFUL of all the Greek city-states. It was also a great center of the arts and learning. Its patron, Athena was goddess of wisdom and warfare and perfectly symbolized the two sides of her city's life. In 480 B.C., the Persians invaded and destroyed the city, including the temples on the Acropolis. Later, when Athens had played a leading role in the Persian wars (pp. 54–55) and successfully defended Greece, a huge rebuilding program was launched by the leader of Athens, Perikles (pp. 18–19). Athens was situated in an area called Attica and was more densely populated than other Greek cities. The people of Athens lived on the land below the Acropolis. Many fine public squares and colonnaded buildings have been found there around the *agora*, an open space for meeting and commercial activity. Nearby was the port of Athens, the Piraeus. Access to the sea was a main reason for Athens' military and economic successes.

THE ACROPOLIS
In early times, the Acropolis (high city) of Athens was a fortified citadel. Later, it became the most sacred part of the town and the site of many important temples and sanctuaries.

SACRED STATUE
The purpose of the procession shown on this frieze (sculptured panel) was to bring a new dress for a sacred wooden statue of Athena at the Acropolis. The dress, a woven *peplos* (pp. 42–43), is being handed to a priest.

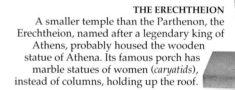

THE ERECHTHEION
A smaller temple than the Parthenon, the Erechtheion, named after a legendary king of Athens, probably housed the wooden statue of Athena. Its famous porch has marble statues of women (*caryatids*), instead of columns, holding up the roof.

THE PARTHENON FRIEZE
The marble frieze of the Parthenon went around all four sides of the temple and was set up high, on the outside of the main building near the ceiling of the colonnade.

Its main subject was the procession of worshipers which wound its way up from the *agora* to the Acropolis every four years as part of the festival called the Great Panathenaea in honor of the goddess Athena. Young men on horseback take up much of the frieze.

THE PARTHENON

The temple of the Parthenon occupies the highest point of the Acropolis. It was dedicated to Athena. The word Parthenon comes from the Greek word *parthenos*, meaning virgin. Athena was sometimes described as Athena Parthenos. The Parthenon, which still stands today, was built between 447 and 432 B.C. The sculptures that decorated it were designed by Pheidias.

GOLDEN GODDESS

Inside the Parthenon stood a huge gold and ivory statue of the goddess Athena, made by the famous sculptor Pheidias, a close friend of Perikles. She appears in all her splendor as goddess of warfare. In this replica based on a smaller copy of the original statue and on descriptions by Greek writers, she wears her *aegis*, a small goatskin cloak fringed with snakes, and a high-crested helmet. On her right hand is a small winged figure of Nike, the goddess of victory.

An Athenian coin showing an owl, the bird of Athena

THE ELGIN MARBLES

Many of the sculptures from the Parthenon were brought to England by Lord Elgin, the British ambassador to the Ottoman court. He saw the sculptures when he visited Athens and was granted permission to bring some back to England. They can be seen today in the British Museum.

Temporary Elgin Room, painted by A. Archer, at the British Museum

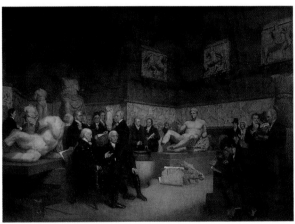

Some young men are trotting gently along, and others are galloping with their cloaks flying out behind them. The background to the frieze was originally painted, probably a bright blue. The horses used to have bridles of bronze.

The bridles have not survived, leaving only traces of the holes where they were attached to the marble. In the south frieze a number of young cows can be seen. In other parts of the frieze are women carrying sacrificial vessels, bowls, and jugs.

Power and politics in Athens

ANCIENT GREECE WAS MADE UP of a number of independent city-states. There were very few rich people and a great number of poor. In early times, tyrants (cruel leaders) and rich landowners controlled the poor. In Athens and some other city-states the tyrants were driven out by the people, who then acquired power and freedom. This new form of government, developed in Athens, was called democracy. The Assembly was the main forum of political life. Meetings took place on a hill called the Pnyx near the Acropolis. All citizens, rich or poor, could make a speech and vote at the Assembly. At least 6,000 people had to be present for a meeting to take place. The Assembly made important decisions - for example, whether or not to declare war. A higher government body consisted of a Council of 500 members, which met in a round building called the *tholos*. In times of war, decisions were made about the defense of the city by a group of ten military commanders called *strategoi*, who were elected annually and could be reelected many times.

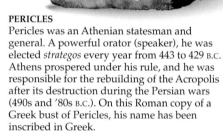

PERICLES

Pericles was an Athenian statesman and general. A powerful orator (speaker), he was elected *strategos* every year from 443 to 429 B.C. Athens prospered under his rule, and he was responsible for the rebuilding of the Acropolis after its destruction during the Persian wars (490s and '80s B.C.). On this Roman copy of a Greek bust of Pericles, his name has been inscribed in Greek.

BOOT BOY

This little bronze figure is of an African boy holding a shoe. Greek society depended on slaves. Some were prisoners of war; some were foreigners bought from slave traders. Most of the housework in wealthy Greek homes was done by slaves. Other heavy work, such as working in the silver mines in southern Greece, was also done by slaves. A few lucky slaves might receive wages from their masters and be able to buy back their freedom. Others, such as the tutors employed to teach the sons of rich families, may have been treated with respect, but most slaves probably led lives of drudgery.

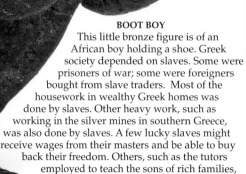

PALACE OF WESTMINSTER

Many modern governments have been influenced by the democratic system that developed in Athens in the fifth century B.C. The word "democracy" is Greek and means "power of the people." Democracy in ancient Greece, however, was different from what it is today - a sizeable chunk of Greek society including women, foreigners, and slaves, did not have the vote.

TREASURY OF TRIUMPH

The battle of Marathon was a famous victory by the Greeks over the Persians in 490 B.C. Soon afterward this fine marble building was erected at Delphi by the Athenians as a symbol of triumph. It was a treasury full of Persian spoils, an expression of the prestige of Athens, and also a religious offering to Apollo at his holiest sanctuary. It stands in a prominent position beside the Sacred Way, which winds up to the temple. The Treasury is a vivid illustration of the close links between religion and politics in the ancient Greek world.

EXILE OF THEMISTOCLES

This coin shows an Athenian leader, Themistocles, whose main achievement was the creation of the fleet that enabled the Greeks to destroy the Persians at the battle of Salamis in 480 B.C. (pp. 54–55). Later, he was banished (sent away) from Athens. When citizens wished to banish a politician, they would write his name on a piece of pottery, an *ostrakon*, which were then counted. If more than 6,000 votes were cast, the politician had to leave Athens for ten years.

WORDS OF BRONZE

This bronze tablet is inscribed with a treaty between the people of Elis and the citizens of Heraea in Arcadia in southern Greece. The treaty was to last 100 years, and the two parties promised to stand by one another, particularly in war. If either party failed to observe the treaty, there was a penalty of a talent of silver (a talent was an ancient unit of weight).

JUDGMENT TABLET

This oblong tablet contains a treaty between the cities of Oeantheia and Chaleion. The two sides agreed that there should be a legal process for solving disputes about the ownership of land, and penalties imposed if the treaty was broken by either side.

Gods, goddesses, and heroes

THE GREEKS BELIEVED that all the gods were descendants of Gaia (the earth) and Uranos (the sky). They thought the gods were probably much like humans: they fell in love with each other, married, quarreled, had children, played music, and in many other ways mirrored human characteristics (or humans mirrored theirs). All the gods had their own spheres of influence. Demeter and Persephone were responsible for the grain growing, Artemis was the goddess of hunting, Apollo could foretell the future, and Aphrodite was the goddess of love. Many of the best-known gods had temples and sanctuaries dedicated to them, and much money and artistic ability were lavished on these places. Religion played a large part in the lives of ordinary people. Indeed, most of the beautiful buildings that still survive are temples. Worshipers believed that the gods would treat them well and meet their needs if they offered them animal sacrifices and the fruits of the harvest.

DIONYSOS FROM DELOS
Dionysos was the god of wine and earth fertility. In this mosaic from the island of Delos, he is riding a tiger.

THE KING OF THE GODS
Zeus was the king of the gods. He usually appears in art as a strong, middle-aged, bearded man of great power and dignity. Sometimes he carries his symbol, a thunderbolt.

HOME OF THE GODS
Mount Olympus is the highest mountain in Greece and was believed to be the home of the gods. It is in the north of Greece, on the borders of Thessaly and Macedonia.

GODDESS OF LOVE
This bronze head of Aphrodite comes from eastern Turkey. The goddess was born from the sea foam and believed to have been carried by the Zephyrs (West Winds) to Cyprus. Although she was married to Hephaistos, she fell in love with Ares, the god of war.

BEAUTY AND THE BEAST
On this mirror case, the goddess Aphrodite is playing a game of knucklebones (pp. 34–35) with the god Pan. The goddess of love and beauty is often shown by artists as a graceful young woman, with the upper part of her body bare. She is accompanied by Eros (according to some myths, her son), shown here as a small, winged boy, and a goose, a symbol associated with her. Pan was a god of the countryside and had goat's legs and ears.

BRAIN CHILD

The strange birth of Athena was a favorite subject for Greek vase painters. She was the daughter of Zeus by the goddess Metis (meaning wisdom). Zeus was told that any child born to Metis would be more powerful than its father, and so, hoping to prevent this, he swallowed Metis. When the time came for Athena to be born, Zeus' head was cut open by the god Hephaistos and Athena emerged.

Apollo and Daphne by Italian artist Antonio Pollaiuolo (1429 -1498)

APOLLO AND DAPHNE

Daphne was a nymph loved by Apollo. According to one myth he tried to seize her, but she escaped. In answer to her prayer, Zeus turned her into a laurel tree – ironically, the tree sacred to Apollo.

HEPHAISTOS

The lame god Hephaistos, who was a blacksmith, made a special ax to cut open Zeus' head. He also made a throne and shield for the king of the gods. He was the god of fire and husband of Aphrodite.

APOLLO

Apollo, a beautiful young deity, was the twin brother of Artemis, the goddess of the hunt. He had a famous shrine and oracle at Delphi. He is associated with the sun, with light, and with healing and medicine.

ATHENA

Athena was the patron goddess of the city of Athens. She was also the goddess of wisdom and warfare and presided over the arts, literature; and philosophy. Her favorite bird was the owl and her favorite plant the olive tree, which she is credited with introducing to Athens. In the Trojan War (pp. 12–13) she fought on the side of the Greeks and assisted Odysseus in his long voyage home.

DEMETER AND PERSEPHONE

Demeter and Persephone, mother and daughter, were goddesses of the grain. This terra-cotta figure shows them sitting side by side wearing headdresses. They were probably holding the reins of an oxcart, which has not survived the years.

Continued on next page

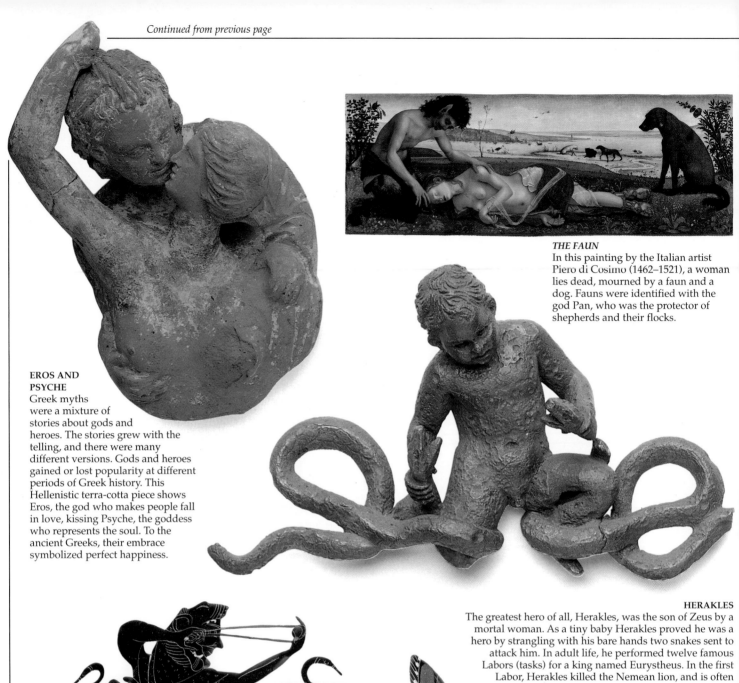

THE FAUN
In this painting by the Italian artist Piero di Cosimo (1462–1521), a woman lies dead, mourned by a faun and a dog. Fauns were identified with the god Pan, who was the protector of shepherds and their flocks.

EROS AND PSYCHE
Greek myths were a mixture of stories about gods and heroes. The stories grew with the telling, and there were many different versions. Gods and heroes gained or lost popularity at different periods of Greek history. This Hellenistic terra-cotta piece shows Eros, the god who makes people fall in love, kissing Psyche, the goddess who represents the soul. To the ancient Greeks, their embrace symbolized perfect happiness.

HERAKLES
The greatest hero of all, Herakles, was the son of Zeus by a mortal woman. As a tiny baby Herakles proved he was a hero by strangling with his bare hands two snakes sent to attack him. In adult life, he performed twelve famous Labors (tasks) for a king named Eurystheus. In the first Labor, Herakles killed the Nemean lion, and is often shown, as on this vase, wearing its skin. The Labor shown here is the killing of the Stymphalian birds. These birds, which lived near a lake in the northeast Peloponnesus, destroyed crops and wounded people with their poisonous feathers. Herakles scared them with a bronze rattle given to him by the smith god Hephaestus (pp. 20–21) and then shot them with a sling. He was strong and fierce but he liked wine and women and had many love affairs.

PEGASUS
This coin shows the winged horse Pegasus. Pegasus was tamed by the hero Bellerophon, who tried to ride him to heaven. But Pegasus was stung by a gadfly sent by Zeus and threw Bellerophon off his back and down to earth.

TOO HIGH!
Icarus was the son of Daedalus, a mythical craftsman who made wings for himself and his son, to enable them to fly. The wings were attached by wax. Icarus flew too high, the heat of the sun melted the wax, and he fell into the Aegean Sea and drowned.

THE BUILDING OF THE ARGO
This Roman terra-cotta wall panel shows a scene from the famous myth of Jason and the Argonauts. Jason was a prince from Thessaly in northern Greece, and the Argonauts were a group of heroes who sailed with him on a ship they had built called the Argo. Heroes are concerned with undertaking long and difficult journeys and freeing mankind from evil, often in the form of strange monsters. Jason and his crew set sail to find the Golden Fleece, which hung on a tree near the Black Sea, guarded by a snake. The goddess Athena helped Jason in this task; she can be seen on the left helping the crew to construct the Argo.

LURE OF THE LYRE
Orpheus was a poet and a musician. He played the lyre and the kithara and sang so well that he could tame wild animals; trees and plants would bend their branches to him, and he could soothe the most violent of tempers. He took part in the expedition of Jason and the Argonauts and calmed the crew and stilled the waves with his music. In this beautiful painting by Dutch artist Roelandt Savery (1576–1639), the magic of Orpheus' music is illustrated. All the birds and beasts are lying down together in an enchanted landscape.

PERSEUS AND MEDUSA
On this vase painting of 460 B.C., the hero Perseus has just cut off the head of the gorgon Medusa. Medusa sinks to the ground with blood spurting from her severed neck. Her head can be seen in Perseus' bag.

Festivals and oracles

COME DANCING
At a festival in the countryside, a row of people join hands and approach an altar where a sacrifice is blazing. A priestess, or perhaps Demeter, the corn goddess, stands behind the altar with a flat basket used for winnowing grain.

Rᴇʟɪɢɪᴏɴ ᴘʟᴀʏᴇᴅ ᴀ ᴍᴀᴊᴏʀ ᴘᴀʀᴛ in Greek life. The Greeks believed that they could strike a bargain with the gods and offered them gold, silver, and animal sacrifice. They also held festivals and games in their honor. In return, they expected the gods to protect them from illness, look after their crops, and grant other favors. Communication with the gods had a regular place in the calendar; most festivals took place once a year, or sometimes every four years. Gods were worshiped in sanctuaries. One of the most important in Greece was that of Apollo at Delphi. He was associated with light and healing, but if he was angry, his arrows could cause plague. He was well known as a god of prophecy, and at Delphi he would reply to questions about the future. His priestess would act as his mouthpiece and make obscure pronouncements that could be interpreted in different ways. The oracle (as these forecasts were called) at Delphi lasted into Christian times.

HOLY BULL
A bull was one of the animals offered at important sacrificial occasions. Bulls would be decorated with garlands of plants and ribbons to show that they had been set aside for the gods. Garlanded bulls' heads were the inspiration for some of the decorative patterns on temples.

SOMETHING OLD, SOMETHING NEW
The huge columns of a Greek temple at ancient Poseidonia (Paestum) in southern Italy frame a bride and groom posing for their wedding photos. Ancient ruins like these are believed to bring good luck to a new marriage.

CENTER OF THE WORLD
Delphi was thought to be the center of the world, at the very point where two birds flying from opposite ends of the earth met. The Greeks placed a huge stone there, the *omphalos*, or navel of the world. Carved on this version, which is in the museum at Delphi, is a network of woolen strands – a sign that this was a holy object.

THE CHARIOTEER

A stadium was built high above the temple to Apollo at Delphi, for games and chariot races in honor of the god. Winning the chariot race was the greatest honor of the games, and the owner of the winning team of horses paid for a statue to celebrate his success.

The eyes of this magnificent bronze statue are inlaid with glass and stone, the lips are copper, and the headband is patterned with silver. The charioteer is still holding the reins of his horses, even though they have long disappeared. This is one of the best-known statues of ancient Greece.

TEMPLE OF APOLLO

Delphi was the home of the main shrine of Apollo. It lies on the steep slopes of Mount Parnassus, the favorite haunt of Apollo and also of the Muses, who looked after the arts and music. A road lined with small buildings (to house the rich gifts made to the god) still winds its way up the slope and past the remains of his great temple, which housed the oracle.

SANCTUARY OF ATHENA

The sanctuary of Athena lies farther down the mountain from Apollo's shrine. In the middle of it is this circular building, the purpose of which is unknown. It is set against the silvery blue background of thousands of olive trees. Athena was supposed to have created the olive tree, and these groves still provide a rich harvest for the local people.

THE WAY TO ATHENA

In the goddess Athena's own city of Athens lay the Panathenaic Way, a special road that led up to her temples and altars on the Acropolis. Leading up from the *agora*, the market and meeting place of the city, the road today passes the rebuilt version of a *stoa*, a long, colonnaded building. It was used for commerce and conversation.

PROCESSION OF SACRIFICE

On this broad bowl used for wine (the ivy leaves that decorate it are linked with Dionysos, the wine god), a long line of people are on their way to worship the goddess Athena. The altar where the flames are already rising is on the right of the bowl. Athena is standing behind the altar. The procession is led by a woman carrying a tray of cakes on her head. She is followed by a man leading the sacrificial bull, then a man playing the double pipes. The rest of the men in the procession carry all the objects necessary for the worship of the goddess, such as a jug of wine. A mule cart brings up the rear.

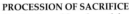

Temples

GREEK LIFE WAS DOMINATED by religion, so it is not surprising that the temples of ancient Greece were the biggest and most beautiful buildings. They also had a political purpose, as they were often built to celebrate civic power and pride or to offer thanks to the patron deity of a city for success in war. Temples were made of limestone or marble, with roofs and ceilings of wood. Roof tiles were made of terra cotta or stone. Large numbers of workers must have been employed in temple construction. Huge stone blocks had to be transported from quarries in ox-drawn carts. These blocks were carved on site by masons using hammers and mallets. The tall columns were made in cylindrical sections ("drums"), held together with metal pegs and lifted into position with ropes and pulleys. Decorative sculpture in the form of friezes and statues in the pediments (the triangular gable ends), added to the grandeur and beauty of Greek temples.

CAPE SOUNION
A fifth-century marble temple to Poseidon, god of the sea, crowns a high promontory south of Athens. It was a landmark for sailors returning home to Athens. The English romantic poet George Gordon, Lord Byron (1788–1824) was very moved by its beauty.

ZEUS' TEMPLE
A great international festival of athletics (pp. 44–45) in honor of Zeus was held every four years at Olympia, a sanctuary on the banks of the Alpheios river. Colossal remains of the great temple of Zeus built in the fifth century, and other important buildings, have been found there.

TEMPLE OF CERES
Poseidonia (later called Paestum) in southern Italy, south of Naples, was a rich Greek colony and has the best preserved ancient temples anywhere in the Greek world. This one, built in the sixth century B.C. in the Doric style and known as the temple of Ceres (the Roman version of Demeter), was in fact dedicated to the goddess Athena and later used as a Christian church. For hundreds of years few people visited the site of Paestum because it was hidden by swamps and undergrowth, and this accounts for the remarkably good condition of the buildings today.

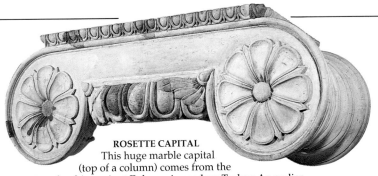

ROSETTE CAPITAL
This huge marble capital (top of a column) comes from the temple of Artemis at Ephesus in modern Turkey. An earlier temple on the same site was destroyed by fire in 356 B.C., on the same night that Alexander the Great (pp. 62–63) was born.

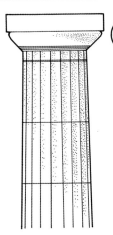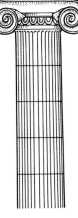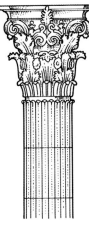

DORIC
The Doric style is sturdy, and its top (the capital) is plain. This style was used in mainland Greece and the colonies in southern Italy and Sicily.

IONIC
The Ionic style is thinner and more elegant. Its capital is decorated with a scroll-like design (a volute). This style was used in eastern Greece and the islands.

CORINTHIAN
The Corinthian style was seldom used in the Greek world, but often appeared in Roman temples. Its capital is elaborate and decorated with acanthus leaves.

LION'S MOUTH
Rain water was sometimes drained away from the roofs of temples through spouts in the form of lions' heads. This one comes from a temple of Athena at Priene, just south of Ephesus, in modern Turkey.

COLUMNS AND CAPITALS
Most Greek buildings had vertical columns and horizontal lintels (beams). This style of construction may have been inspired by earlier wooden buildings whose roofs were supported by tree trunks.

CORINTHIAN CAPITAL
This Corinthian capital once decorated a gracious colonnaded building in Asia Minor (modern Turkey). The face is a version of a female theatrical mask. The deeply carved leaves below copy those of the acanthus plant, a favorite design of Greek artists. The plant is easily identified by its spreading, leathery leaves.

PALMETTE ROOF TILE
The end of this roof tile is decorated with a palmette shape. It comes from a temple to Apollo at Bassae in southern Greece. This area was famous for its fighting men, and Apollo may have been worshiped here as a god of soldiers.

LOTUS LEAVES
This marble fragment is crisply carved with a frieze of lotus and palmette designs and other delicate moldings. It comes from the top part of the east wall of the temple of the Erechtheion on the Acropolis of Athens (pp. 16–17). The roof of the south porch of the building is supported by columns in the form of standing women with baskets on their heads. Pericles ordered the construction of the Erechtheion (which survives today on the site of older buildings) in the middle fifth century B.C. to beautify the city of Athens.

At home

THE GREEKS LIKED THEIR HOMES to be private. The windows were small and set high in the walls, which were made from sun-dried mud bricks which have not survived well. This farmhouse is a fairly simple building; town houses probably had more rooms and were more luxurious. The garden or courtyard was in the middle of the house and all the rooms were arranged around it. There might have been a well in the courtyard, where slave girls did the family washing and filled the water pots. In the porch stood a herm, a statue of the god Hermes which prevented evil spirits from entering. It is difficult to know exactly what a Greek home looked like. This farmhouse model is based on information gathered from excavating a house in the country to the south of Athens, which was occupied in the fourth century B.C.

Terra-cotta figurine shows a woman grinding grain to make bread

DOORS AND JARS
Wood was expensive in Greece, and doors were therefore precious objects. Two bowls on stands, used in wedding rituals, can be seen in front.

RAIN CAT
Some wealthier homes had gutters on the roofs for the removal of rainwater. The water flowed onto the ground through water spouts like this one, which is shaped like a lion's head.

Ladder to upper story

Every house had an altar, where the family would offer sacrifices to the gods

The women's quarters (gynaeceum) housed the weaving looms, babies' cradles, and couches

Hearth for cooking and providing burning charcoal for portable braziers

The dining room (andron), where the men entertained their friends

ON THE TILES
Sometimes the ends of terra-cotta roof tiles on temples and wealthier homes were decorated with human and animal faces. This gorgon head has tight curls and a protruding tongue. Originally it would have been brightly colored and clearly visible from the ground.

SITTING PRETTY
In this vase painting, a young woman, perhaps a bride preparing for her wedding, is sitting on a chair in her house. This elegant chair shape is often seen on Greek vases.

COUCHES
As Greek couches were made mainly of wood, none have survived. This bronze decoration was once fitted onto a couch near the head rest. Similar couches were used at mealtimes.

Roof made of clay tiles

Walls made of mud bricks, sometimes plastered over

Window openings without glass but with wooden shutters

Stone foundations were often stolen by builders centuries later

Wooden door with bronze fittings

In the country a stone wall usually surrounded the property

Women's world

THE LIVES OF WOMEN in ancient Greece were restricted. Women were very much under the control of their husbands, fathers, or brothers, and rarely took part in politics or any form of public life. Most women could not inherit property and were allowed very little money. A girl would marry very young, at the age of 13 or 14. Her husband, who was certain to be much older, was chosen for her by her father. The main purpose of marriage was to have a baby, preferably a boy, to carry on the male line. The status of a woman greatly increased when she had given birth to a boy (pp. 32–33). Some marriages seem to have been happy. A number of tombstones have survived that commemorate women who died in childbirth. There are tender inscriptions from the grieving husbands. It is possible that, although legally they had very little freedom, some women could make important decisions about family life. Their spinning and weaving work made an important contribution to the household.

Greek Woman by British artist Sir Lawrence Alma-Tadema (1836-1912)

SPINDLE
Wool was spun into yarn with a spindle. This one is made of wood, but bronze and bone examples also exist. At one end is a weight, known as a spindle whorl. The spindle twirls around and spins the wool fiber into thread.

HOMEMAKERS
Girls in Greece did not go to school (pp. 32–33). Instead, they stayed at home and were taught by their mothers how to spin and weave and look after the house. Some wealthier women were taught to read and write. On this vase a woman is reading from a papyrus scroll.

SPINNER
On this white-ground jug a woman is spinning with both a distaff and spindle. The distaff was a shaft of wood or metal with a spike at one end and a handle at the other.

WELL WOMEN
Few houses had their own private wells, and in Athens women and slave girls went to public fountains to fill their water pots. The water spout at this fountain is shaped like a lion's head. The women wait their turn, their water pots balanced on their heads. This was a good opportunity to meet with friends and chat.

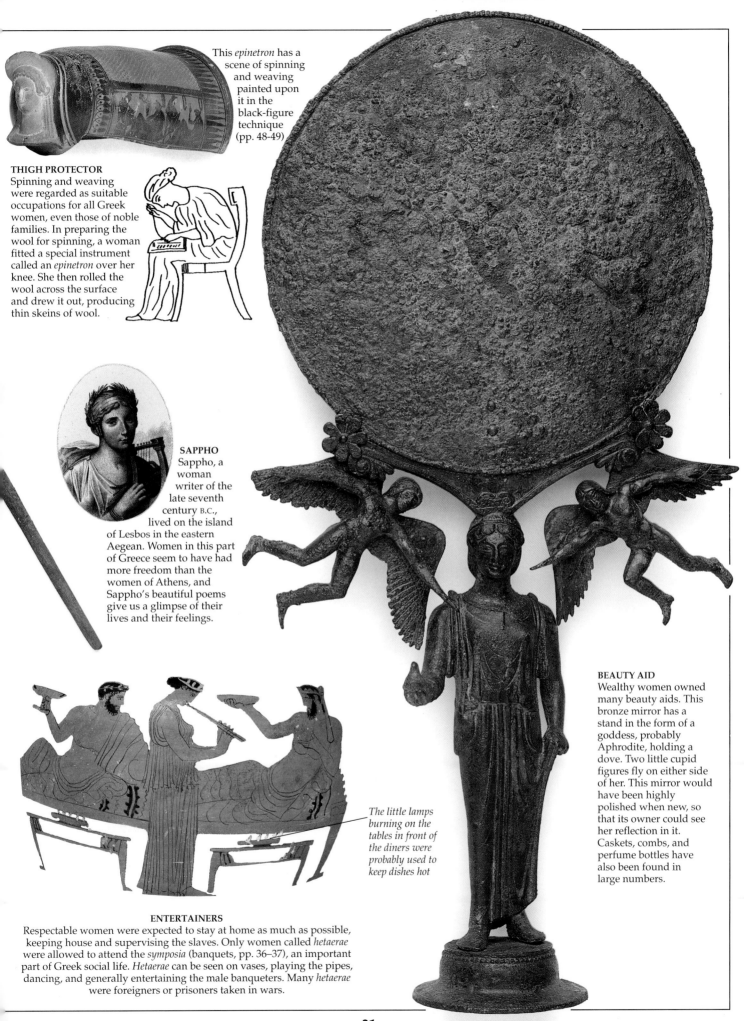

This *epinetron* has a scene of spinning and weaving painted upon it in the black-figure technique (pp. 48-49)

THIGH PROTECTOR
Spinning and weaving were regarded as suitable occupations for all Greek women, even those of noble families. In preparing the wool for spinning, a woman fitted a special instrument called an *epinetron* over her knee. She then rolled the wool across the surface and drew it out, producing thin skeins of wool.

SAPPHO
Sappho, a woman writer of the late seventh century B.C., lived on the island of Lesbos in the eastern Aegean. Women in this part of Greece seem to have had more freedom than the women of Athens, and Sappho's beautiful poems give us a glimpse of their lives and their feelings.

The little lamps burning on the tables in front of the diners were probably used to keep dishes hot

ENTERTAINERS
Respectable women were expected to stay at home as much as possible, keeping house and supervising the slaves. Only women called *hetaerae* were allowed to attend the *symposia* (banquets, pp. 36–37), an important part of Greek social life. *Hetaerae* can be seen on vases, playing the pipes, dancing, and generally entertaining the male banqueters. Many *hetaerae* were foreigners or prisoners taken in wars.

BEAUTY AID
Wealthy women owned many beauty aids. This bronze mirror has a stand in the form of a goddess, probably Aphrodite, holding a dove. Two little cupid figures fly on either side of her. This mirror would have been highly polished when new, so that its owner could see her reflection in it. Caskets, combs, and perfume bottles have also been found in large numbers.

31

Growing up in Greece

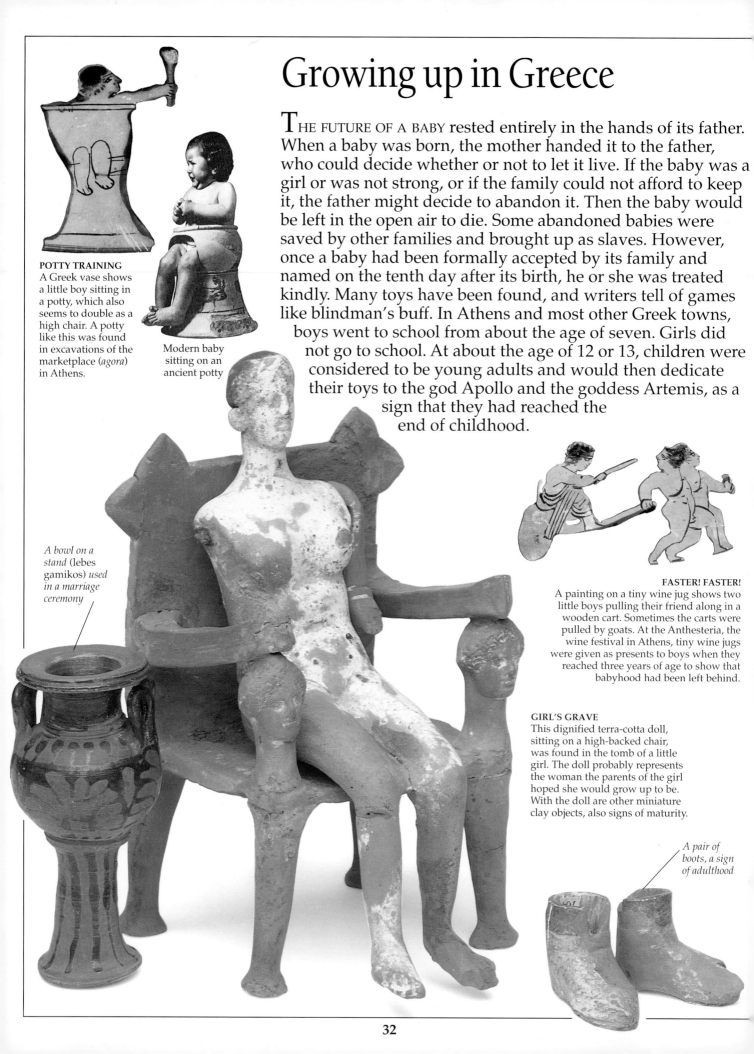

The FUTURE OF A BABY rested entirely in the hands of its father. When a baby was born, the mother handed it to the father, who could decide whether or not to let it live. If the baby was a girl or was not strong, or if the family could not afford to keep it, the father might decide to abandon it. Then the baby would be left in the open air to die. Some abandoned babies were saved by other families and brought up as slaves. However, once a baby had been formally accepted by its family and named on the tenth day after its birth, he or she was treated kindly. Many toys have been found, and writers tell of games like blindman's buff. In Athens and most other Greek towns, boys went to school from about the age of seven. Girls did not go to school. At about the age of 12 or 13, children were considered to be young adults and would then dedicate their toys to the god Apollo and the goddess Artemis, as a sign that they had reached the end of childhood.

POTTY TRAINING
A Greek vase shows a little boy sitting in a potty, which also seems to double as a high chair. A potty like this was found in excavations of the marketplace (*agora*) in Athens.

Modern baby sitting on an ancient potty

A bowl on a stand (lebes gamikos) used in a marriage ceremony

FASTER! FASTER!
A painting on a tiny wine jug shows two little boys pulling their friend along in a wooden cart. Sometimes the carts were pulled by goats. At the Anthesteria, the wine festival in Athens, tiny wine jugs were given as presents to boys when they reached three years of age to show that babyhood had been left behind.

GIRL'S GRAVE
This dignified terra-cotta doll, sitting on a high-backed chair, was found in the tomb of a little girl. The doll probably represents the woman the parents of the girl hoped she would grow up to be. With the doll are other miniature clay objects, also signs of maturity.

A pair of boots, a sign of adulthood

Education

When boys went to school at seven, they learned reading, writing, and arithmetic from a teacher called a *grammatistes*. They learned music, including the playing of an instrument, from a teacher known as a *kitharistes*. They also had to memorize poetry and learn the art of debating. Older boys were taught by teachers called Sophists. Sophists traveled from town to town and often taught their students in the *gymnasia*, or training grounds. Girls did not go to school, but some girls from well-off families had private tutors who taught them to read and write. From their mothers they learned spinning, weaving, and how to run a home.

WAX SCRATCHER
Wooden tablets covered in wax were used in the classroom. Letters were formed in the softened wax with a stylus like this one, usually made of bone or metal. The blunt end was used for smoothing out mistakes.

MINDER
Boys from wealthy families were taken to school by a slave called a *paidogogus*, who, in this vase scene, sits behind the pupil and holds a long staff. The boy stands in front of his teacher, who reads from a papyrus scroll.

TRAINING FOR WAR
Traditionally, boys needed to be fit and strong so that they would grow up to be good soldiers. Therefore, there were special teachers of physical exercise called *paidotribai* (*paidotribes* in the singular). *Paidotribai* taught their pupils athletics and wrestling in the *palaistra*, a long low building with dressing rooms and a colonnaded courtyard covered with sand. All Greek towns had a *palaistra*.

The *palaistra* at Olympia

CLAY COMPANY
Toys for children were often made of wood or fabric, which have not survived. Children also played with clay figurines, perhaps made by potters from leftover clay. These riders were modeled by hand, brightly painted, and then placed in the graves of children to keep them company in the afterlife.

Man riding on goose

Man riding on horse

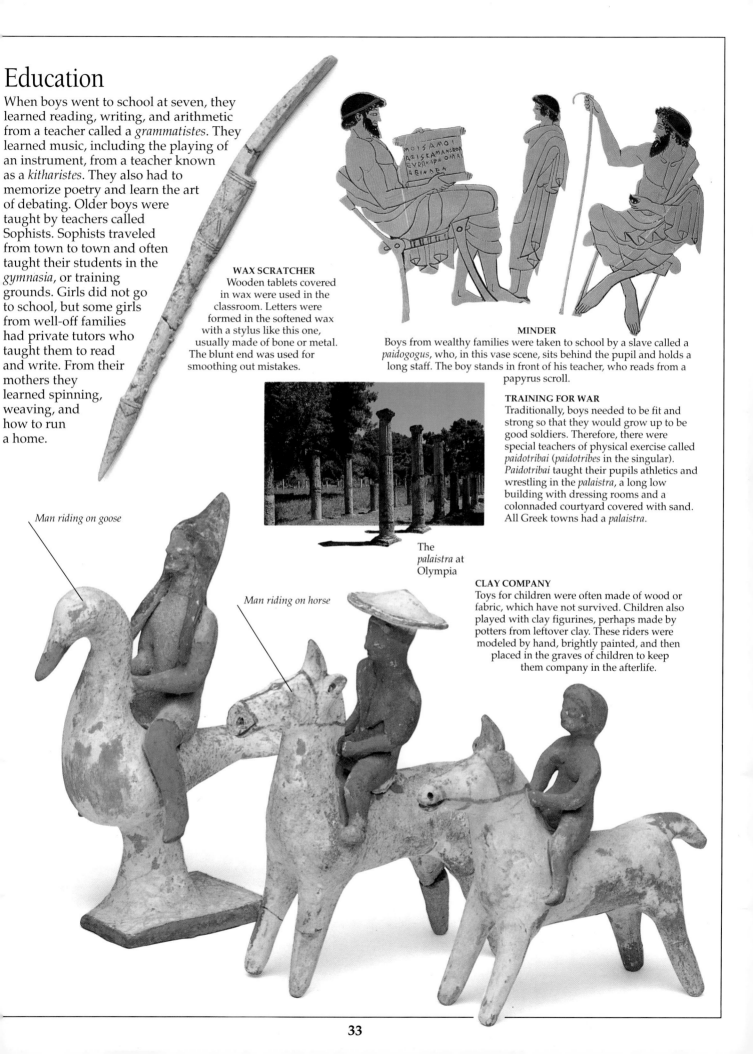

Fun and games

Wealthier greeks, especially those who lived in towns, had plenty of leisure time to spend talking, giving dinner parties, visiting the gymnasium, and playing all kinds of games. Music was particularly important. Greeks sang songs at births, weddings, and funerals. They had love songs, battle songs, drinking songs, and songs of thanksgiving to the gods to celebrate the harvest. There were also many musical instruments: stringed instruments like the harp, the lyre, and the kithara (a kind of lyre), and wind instruments like the syrinx, or panpipes, made of reeds of different lengths. Unfortunately, almost no written music has survived from ancient Greece. Perhaps we can guess what the music may have sounded like by looking at the way women dance on Greek vases. They seem to be moving rhythmically to slow and haunting tunes. Greek men did not dance, but they liked to watch dancers perform at celebrations and drinking parties (pp. 36–37).

DANCING GIRL
This slave girl, wearing a short pleated skirt, is dancing while playing the castanets. She is probably an entertainer at a party.

CLASH OF CYMBALS
This pair of bronze cymbals is inscribed with the name of their owner, Oata. Few musical instruments have survived, but they can often be seen in vase paintings.

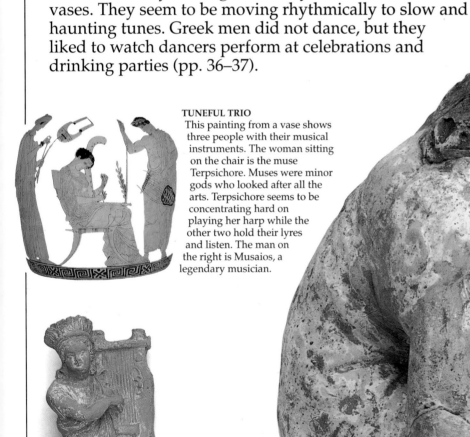

TUNEFUL TRIO
This painting from a vase shows three people with their musical instruments. The woman sitting on the chair is the muse Terpsichore. Muses were minor gods who looked after all the arts. Terpsichore seems to be concentrating hard on playing her harp while the other two hold their lyres and listen. The man on the right is Musaios, a legendary musician.

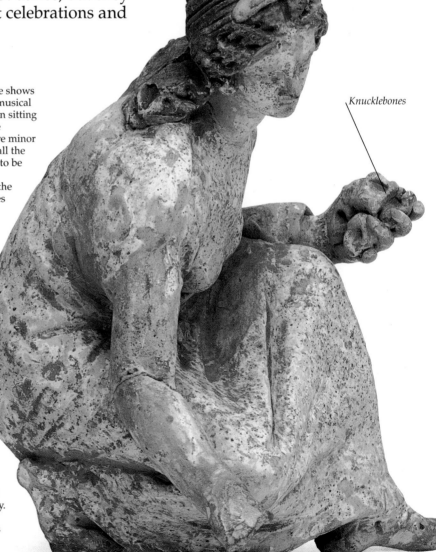

Knucklebones

LARGE LYRE
The kithara, which this woman is playing, is a larger, wooden version of the lyre. She is plucking the strings with a plectrum, similar to the pick used by guitarists today. The kithara was usually played by professional musicians. This figure was made in a town settled by Greeks in southern Italy. Perhaps the woman is singing or chanting poetry as she plays.

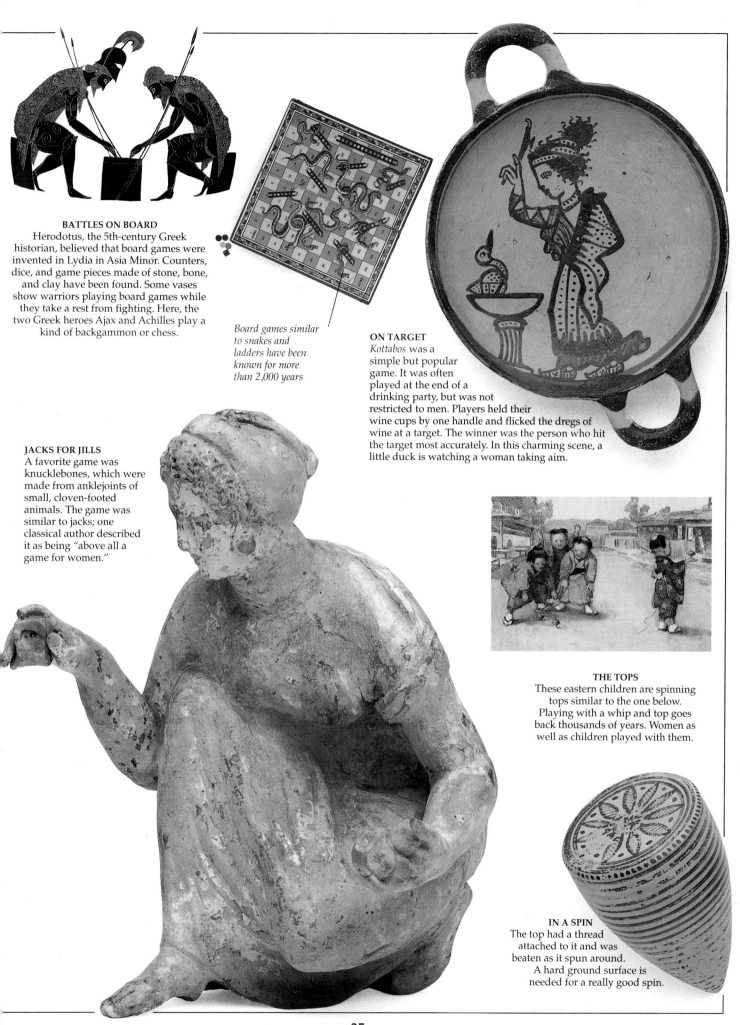

BATTLES ON BOARD
Herodotus, the 5th-century Greek historian, believed that board games were invented in Lydia in Asia Minor. Counters, dice, and game pieces made of stone, bone, and clay have been found. Some vases show warriors playing board games while they take a rest from fighting. Here, the two Greek heroes Ajax and Achilles play a kind of backgammon or chess.

Board games similar to snakes and ladders have been known for more than 2,000 years

ON TARGET
Kottabos was a simple but popular game. It was often played at the end of a drinking party, but was not restricted to men. Players held their wine cups by one handle and flicked the dregs of wine at a target. The winner was the person who hit the target most accurately. In this charming scene, a little duck is watching a woman taking aim.

JACKS FOR JILLS
A favorite game was knucklebones, which were made from anklejoints of small, cloven-footed animals. The game was similar to jacks; one classical author described it as being "above all a game for women."

THE TOPS
These eastern children are spinning tops similar to the one below. Playing with a whip and top goes back thousands of years. Women as well as children played with them.

IN A SPIN
The top had a thread attached to it and was beaten as it spun around. A hard ground surface is needed for a really good spin.

Wining and dining

DIVER'S TOMB
A typical banqueting scene is painted on the wall of a tomb (p. 60) at Paestum, a Greek colony in Italy. It shows young men reclining together on couches, while slaves serve food and wine on small tables.

Iɴ ATHENS AND OTHER GREEK CITIES, men often held banquets or drinking parties (*symposia*) for their male friends. Some were small, private *symposia*; others were large-scale and public. Private *symposia* took place at home in the dining room (*andron*), which was set aside for the men's use after the evening meal. Many Greek vases show *symposia* scenes. All respectable women were excluded from a *symposion*, but slave girls called *hetaerae* would entertain the men with their dancing, flute playing, and acrobatic displays (pp. 30–31). The evening began with the pouring of libations (usually wine) and the singing of special songs or hymns to the gods. The guests wore garlands and perfume. Early in the evening they might discuss politics and philosophy, but as they drank more and more wine, they would tell jokes, riddles, and stories. Eventually, after drinking a great deal of wine, the banqueters would fall asleep on their comfortable couches, leaving the women and slave boys to tidy up.

DRINKING CUP
This is a special kind of drinking cup used at a *symposion*. It is in the form of a ram's head, and the rim is painted with a banqueting scene of guests leaning back on cushioned couches. It gives us a clear impression of the elegant and comfortable life-style that wealthy Athenian men enjoyed. The cup has no base and was probably passed around from hand to hand.

Olives are plentiful in Greece, and bowls of olives, both green and black, would be offered at a *symposion*, possibly as an appetizer

WINE VESSELS
Wine was the Greeks' favorite drink. It was drunk by everybody, not just the rich, and was usually diluted with water. Bread dipped in wine, eaten with a few figs, was a typical Greek breakfast. Many different kinds of wine container have survived, often made of clay, sometimes of bronze. The big bronze vessel on the far left was used for mixing water and wine together. The mixture would then have been transferred to the jug with the ladle, and the slave would fill his master's cup.

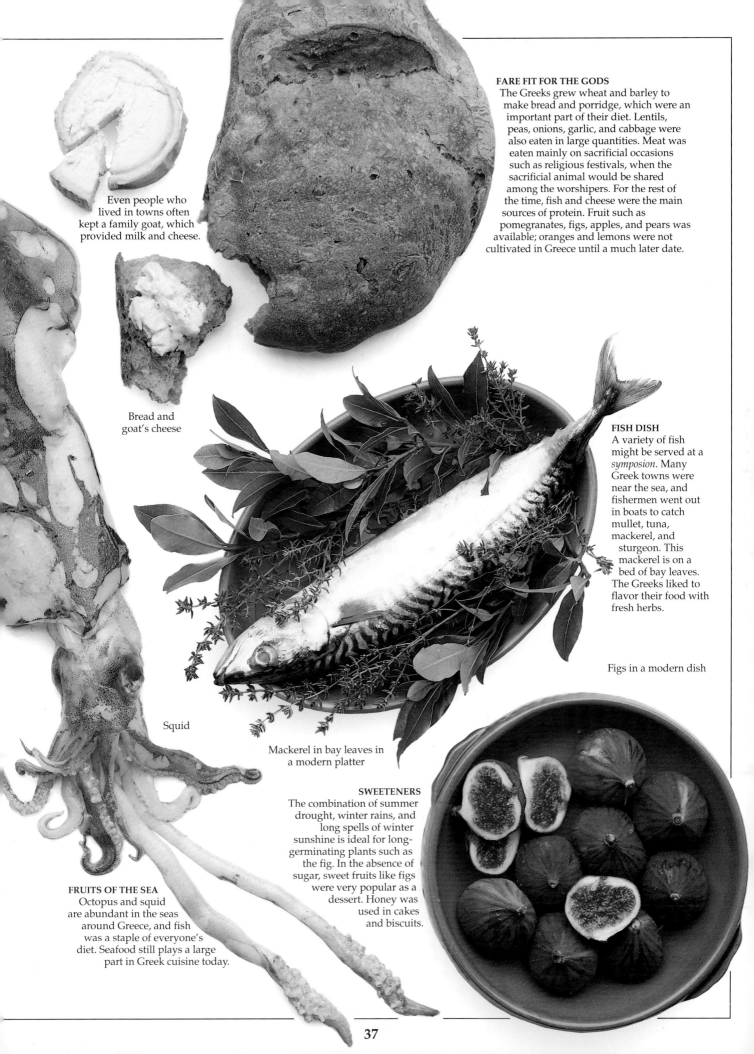

Even people who
lived in towns often
kept a family goat, which
provided milk and cheese.

FARE FIT FOR THE GODS
The Greeks grew wheat and barley to
make bread and porridge, which were an
important part of their diet. Lentils,
peas, onions, garlic, and cabbage were
also eaten in large quantities. Meat was
eaten mainly on sacrificial occasions
such as religious festivals, when the
sacrificial animal would be shared
among the worshipers. For the rest of
the time, fish and cheese were the main
sources of protein. Fruit such as
pomegranates, figs, apples, and pears was
available; oranges and lemons were not
cultivated in Greece until a much later date.

Bread and
goat's cheese

FISH DISH
A variety of fish
might be served at a
symposion. Many
Greek towns were
near the sea, and
fishermen went out
in boats to catch
mullet, tuna,
mackerel, and
sturgeon. This
mackerel is on a
bed of bay leaves.
The Greeks liked to
flavor their food with
fresh herbs.

Figs in a modern dish

Squid

Mackerel in bay leaves in
a modern platter

SWEETENERS
The combination of summer
drought, winter rains, and
long spells of winter
sunshine is ideal for long-
germinating plants such as
the fig. In the absence of
sugar, sweet fruits like figs
were very popular as a
dessert. Honey was
used in cakes
and biscuits.

FRUITS OF THE SEA
Octopus and squid
are abundant in the seas
around Greece, and fish
was a staple of everyone's
diet. Seafood still plays a large
part in Greek cuisine today.

A day out

GREEK THEATERS ARE AMONG the most spectacular buildings that survive from ancient times. In cities like Athens or at sacred sites like Delphi and Epidaurus, people flocked to see dramas in honor of the gods. In Athens, performances for the wine god Dionysus developed into what are now known as plays. From the middle of the sixth century B.C., these plays were organized as competitions and were put on during the spring festival of Dionysus. By the fifth century B.C., both tragedies and comedies were performed and many have survived to the present time. Audiences in Athens spent days watching the plays, seated in the theater of Dionysus on the slope of the Acropolis. All of the actors were men, taking the female parts as well, and no more than three main actors could speak to each other at one time. A larger group of actors, the chorus, commented on the play's action and addressed the audience more directly. Music accompanied the plays, which were acted out on a flat circular area called the orchestra. Women were probably not allowed to go to the theater at all.

TIRED OUT
This small terra-cotta figure shows a comic actor dressed as an old woman. He wears a mask with a wrinkled face and crinkly hair that he has pushed back on his head, as he rests wearily on a seat.

BIRD'S EYE VIEW
From high up in the back row at Epidaurus you can get a clear view of the performance. Here, a temporary set has been built for the modern production of a play.

EURIPIDES
The expression on this sculpture reflects the serious subjects dealt with by the Athenian playwright Euripides. Some of his plays were about the horrors of war, which upset the Athenians because they hinted at Athens' savage treatment of her enemies.

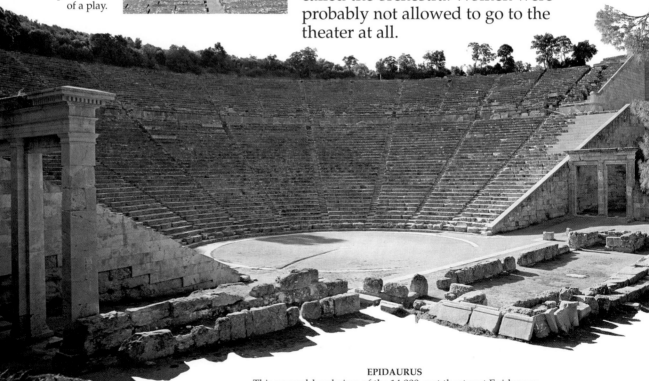

EPIDAURUS
This ground-level view of the 14,000-seat theater at Epidaurus gives an idea of what it is like to be an actor going into the performing area. The carefully curved auditorium (*theatron*, or viewing theater) is a huge semicircular bowl cut into the surface of the hillside. Its shape is not just designed for excellent viewing; sound, too, is caught and amplified, and actors speaking in the orchestra can be heard in the back row.

SOPHOCLES

Portraits of famous playwrights were produced some time after their death, so they were not true likenesses. But these sculptures honored the memory of great writers like the playwright Sophocles. This print decorates a 19th-century text of the plays. Sophocles' plays about royal or legendary families and their tragic lives, like those of King Oedipus or Electra, daughter of Agamemnon, still grip audiences today.

GREEK DRAMA ALIVE AND WELL

A group of actors from Britain's Royal National Theatre perform three plays called *The Oresteia*, by the Athenian playwright Aeschylus. They tell of the death of Agamemnon after the Trojan War and how his son Orestes avenged him.

The elaborate hat is a sign that this bearded man's wealth was not acquired honestly

The muse holds a mask portraying a young woman, one of the characters in a Greek comedy from the fourth century B.C.

SOUVENIR STATUETTES

Statuettes in terra cotta, originally painted in bright colors, are perhaps souvenirs of theater visits. Sets of the entire casts of plays have been found in graves. The graceful female figure is probably a muse, one of the nine guardians of the arts in Greek mythology. The terra cotta of the bearded actor represents a sinister figure from later Greek comedy, who lived off the earnings of *hetaerae*.

Body beautiful

BEAUTY AND CLEANLINESS were important to the ancient Greeks. In sculpture and on vases, men and women can be seen standing in graceful poses and wearing elegant, flowing garments (pp. 42–43). Young men took excellent care of their bodies, keeping fit and strong so that they could be good soldiers and athletes. Nudity was considered quite normal for young men, who always competed naked at the Games (pp. 44–45). After exercise, men and boys rubbed themselves with olive oil to keep their skin supple. Women kept their whole body clothed, and wore something on their head when they went out. Their clothes were so finely spun, however, that they were sometimes almost transparent, and must have been light and cool in the heat of summer. Women wore perfumed oils and tried to keep out of the sun as much as possible, because a suntan was not considered attractive. Wealthy women owned jewelry, much of it in gold and silver and very ornate.

THE AEGINA TREASURE
This gold earring is one of a pair that was found, with a pendant, on the island of Aegina. It was made in Minoan times (pp. 8–9). The circular shape is a snake, and inside it are two dogs standing on the heads of monkeys.

DECORATION IN DEATH
Jewelry was an indication of wealth and prosperity. On this grave carving, a slave is shown handing a bracelet to a woman, probably the dead person herself.

FOLLOWER OF FASHION
This terra-cotta figurine shows a fashionable Greek woman wearing a tunic (*chiton*) and *himation* (cloak; pp. 42-43). She is holding a fan. Clothes were often brightly colored, as can be seen from the traces of paint that remain on the statuette. Hairstyles were very elaborate, and this woman is also wearing some kind of head decoration. Many figures like this have been found at Tanagra in central Greece.

POWDER POT
Women used a special round, flat pot, called a *pyxis*, to hold their perfumes and cosmetics. These pots were sometimes decorated with scenes of women spinning and weaving.

BATH TIME
Greeks bathed regularly. This terra cotta shows that Greek bathtubs were smaller than most modern ones. At the feet end of this tub was a hollow where the water was deeper so that the woman could splash it backward over her body.

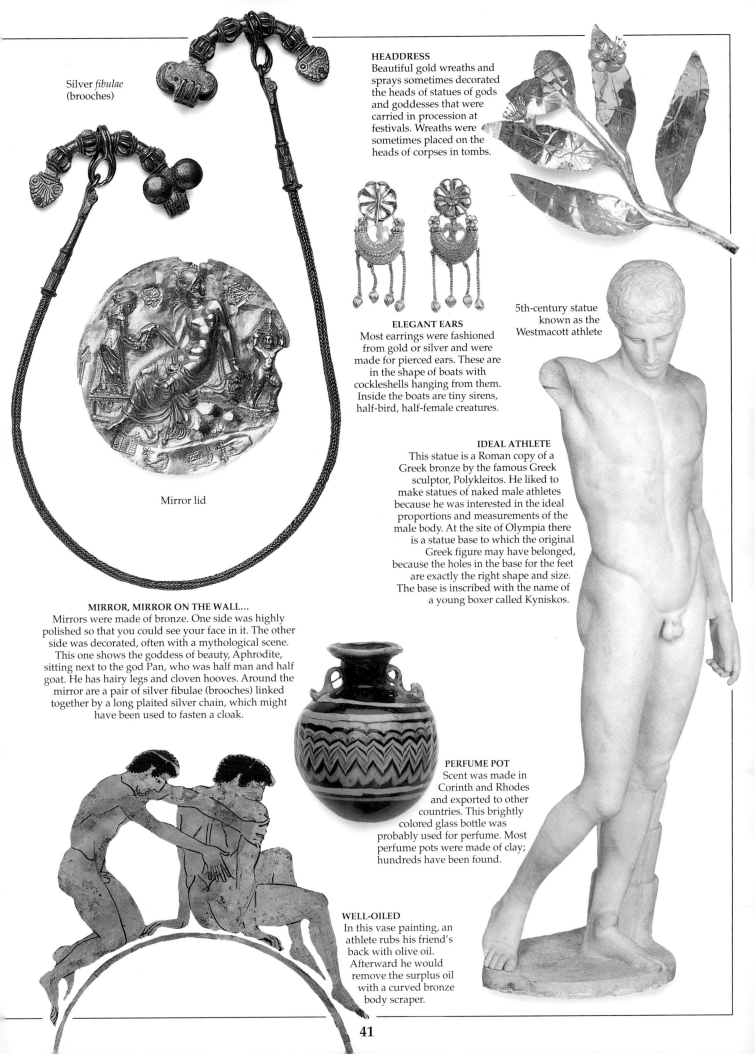

Silver *fibulae*
(brooches)

HEADDRESS
Beautiful gold wreaths and sprays sometimes decorated the heads of statues of gods and goddesses that were carried in procession at festivals. Wreaths were sometimes placed on the heads of corpses in tombs.

ELEGANT EARS
Most earrings were fashioned from gold or silver and were made for pierced ears. These are in the shape of boats with cockleshells hanging from them. Inside the boats are tiny sirens, half-bird, half-female creatures.

5th-century statue known as the Westmacott athlete

Mirror lid

IDEAL ATHLETE
This statue is a Roman copy of a Greek bronze by the famous Greek sculptor, Polykleitos. He liked to make statues of naked male athletes because he was interested in the ideal proportions and measurements of the male body. At the site of Olympia there is a statue base to which the original Greek figure may have belonged, because the holes in the base for the feet are exactly the right shape and size. The base is inscribed with the name of a young boxer called Kyniskos.

MIRROR, MIRROR ON THE WALL...
Mirrors were made of bronze. One side was highly polished so that you could see your face in it. The other side was decorated, often with a mythological scene. This one shows the goddess of beauty, Aphrodite, sitting next to the god Pan, who was half man and half goat. He has hairy legs and cloven hooves. Around the mirror are a pair of silver fibulae (brooches) linked together by a long plaited silver chain, which might have been used to fasten a cloak.

PERFUME POT
Scent was made in Corinth and Rhodes and exported to other countries. This brightly colored glass bottle was probably used for perfume. Most perfume pots were made of clay; hundreds have been found.

WELL-OILED
In this vase painting, an athlete rubs his friend's back with olive oil. Afterward he would remove the surplus oil with a curved bronze body scraper.

Clothes for comfort

GREEK CLOTHES WERE MADE of wool provided by local sheep. The wool was spun very finely so that garments were thinner than modern woolen clothing. Lighter, linen clothes made out of spun flax were also worn. Very wealthy people bought expensive silks from the East, and in Hellenistic times, mulberry trees, food for silkworms, were planted on the island of Kos to start a local silk industry. Bright colors were popular, especially among women. Purple was obtained from sea snails, and a violet shade from an insect larva called the kermes worm. Other dyes came from plants. Poorer people wore undyed clothes. The shapes of clothes were similar for both sexes and hardly changed over hundreds of years. The basic dress was a straight *chiton* (tunic) fastened at the shoulder with brooches or pins; a cloak was flung over the top.

LADY HAMILTON
Sir William Hamilton, British ambassador to Naples in the late 18th century, was a collector of Greek antiquities. His wife, Emma, often dressed in Greek costume.

HAIR DRESSING
Greek women (except slave women) wore their hair long. This woman's style was fashionable in the Classical period. The hair is piled up at the back of the head and held in place with a net and ribbons. Headbands and other gold hair decorations were worn on special occasions.

WRAP UP
Greek underwear was not fitted, but, like outer clothes, was wrapped around the body. On this vase a woman wearing a strip of material as a bra is putting her *chiton* over her head.

READY TO WEAR
The *chiton* was said to have been invented in the Greek colony of Ionia. It was made from a single rectangle of cloth, cut into two and fastened at intervals from neck to elbows to give a graceful loose-sleeve effect. It was gathered at the waist with a belt. The *chiton* shown here is made out of modern woolen fabric that is perhaps slightly thicker and fuller than the original material would have been, in the fifth century B.C. Another, earlier kind of *chiton*, sometimes called a *peplos*, originated in mainland Greece. It did not have sleeves and was secured with with big pins on the shoulders.

Chiton

Chiton

GREEK FANTASY
Sir Lawrence Alma-Tadema (pp. 30–31) often chose Classical subjects for his paintings. The architecture and clothing, however, frequently owed more to his imagination than to historical accuracy.

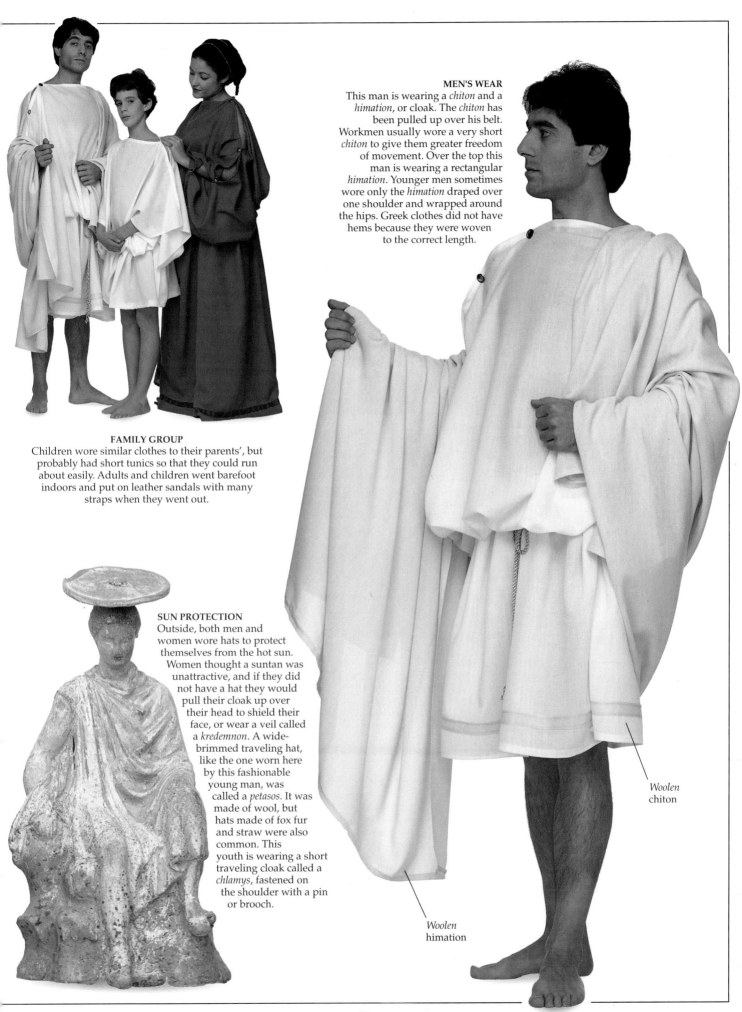

MEN'S WEAR
This man is wearing a *chiton* and a *himation*, or cloak. The *chiton* has been pulled up over his belt. Workmen usually wore a very short *chiton* to give them greater freedom of movement. Over the top this man is wearing a rectangular *himation*. Younger men sometimes wore only the *himation* draped over one shoulder and wrapped around the hips. Greek clothes did not have hems because they were woven to the correct length.

FAMILY GROUP
Children wore similar clothes to their parents', but probably had short tunics so that they could run about easily. Adults and children went barefoot indoors and put on leather sandals with many straps when they went out.

SUN PROTECTION
Outside, both men and women wore hats to protect themselves from the hot sun. Women thought a suntan was unattractive, and if they did not have a hat they would pull their cloak up over their head to shield their face, or wear a veil called a *kredemnon*. A wide-brimmed traveling hat, like the one worn here by this fashionable young man, was called a *petasos*. It was made of wool, but hats made of fox fur and straw were also common. This youth is wearing a short traveling cloak called a *chlamys*, fastened on the shoulder with a pin or brooch.

Woolen chiton

Woolen himation

The Greek games

CHAMPIONS
This fourth-century B.C. bronze statue of a boy jockey and his victorious horse shows the difficulties of racing in ancient Greece. Jockeys, who were usually paid servants of the horse's owner, rode without stirrups.

THE GREEKS BELIEVED IN THE VALUE of sports as training for warfare and as a way of honoring the gods. There were many local sporting competitions, and four big athletic festivals that attracted men from all over the Greek world. Of these, the most important was the Olympic Games, held at Olympia every four years in honor of Zeus. Success in the Games brought honor to the athlete's family and to his hometown, and some successful athletes acquired almost mythical status. Wars were sometimes suspended to allow people to travel in safety to and from Olympia. Many beautiful temples and other buildings that provided facilities for athletes and spectators have been excavated there. The Games went on into Roman times, coming to an end late in the fourth century. In Athens, there were also the Panathenaic Games, which were held every four years in honor of Athena as part of her religious festival; they were an important public holiday. Discipline in sports was strict, and rule breakers were punished severely.

TRAINING TIME
Wrestling, although popular, was regarded as one of the most dangerous of Greek sports. Tripping your opponent was permitted, but biting or gouging out his eyes was strictly forbidden. The man on the left of this statue base is in a racing start position, and the man on the right is testing his javelin.

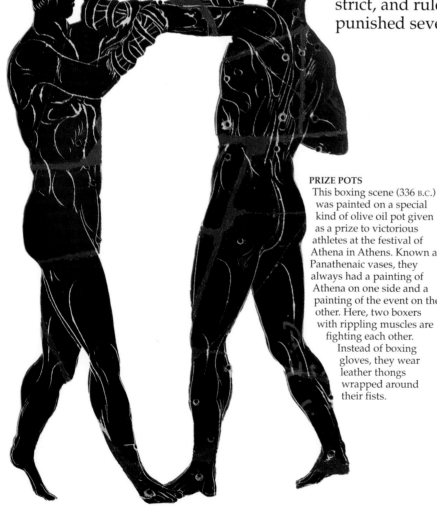

PRIZE POTS
This boxing scene (336 B.C.) was painted on a special kind of olive oil pot given as a prize to victorious athletes at the festival of Athena in Athens. Known as Panathenaic vases, they always had a painting of Athena on one side and a painting of the event on the other. Here, two boxers with rippling muscles are fighting each other. Instead of boxing gloves, they wear leather thongs wrapped around their fists.

THE DELPHI STADIUM
The stadium at Delphi is in the highest part of the ancient city. The stone starting grooves on the track survive, as well as many of the seats, particularly those cut into the mountain side. The stadium could hold 7,000 spectators.

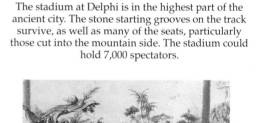

THE OLYMPIC SPIRIT
The spirit of the Olympic Games has greatly inspired artists. This 19th-century German picture depicts naked athletes exercising against a background of classical columns.

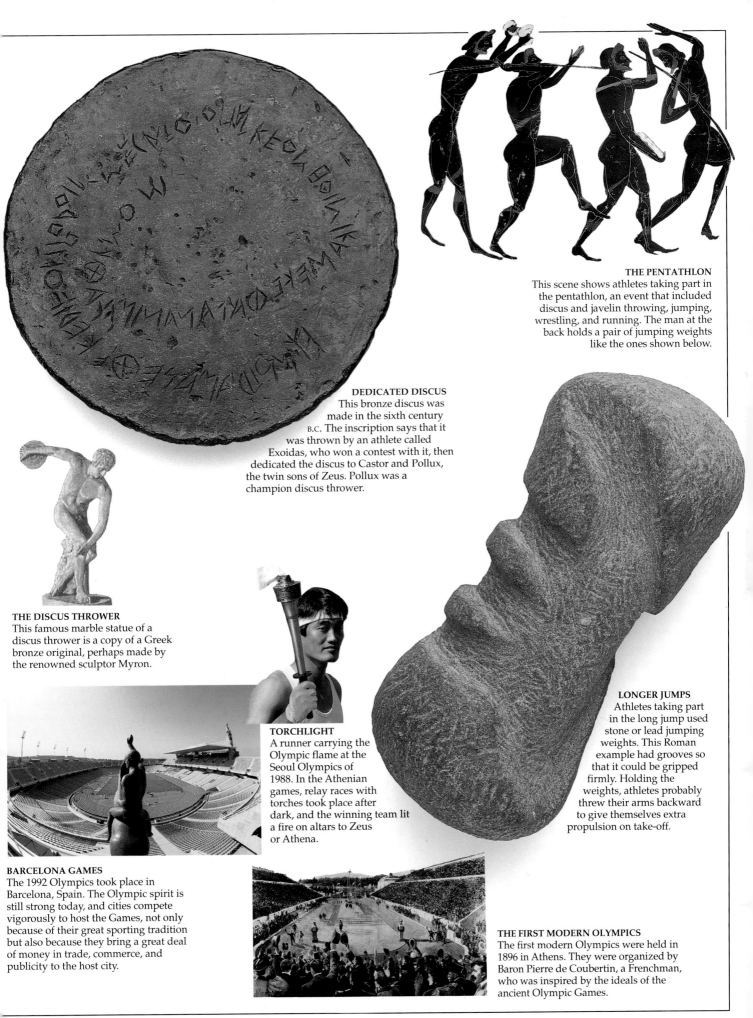

THE PENTATHLON
This scene shows athletes taking part in the pentathlon, an event that included discus and javelin throwing, jumping, wrestling, and running. The man at the back holds a pair of jumping weights like the ones shown below.

DEDICATED DISCUS
This bronze discus was made in the sixth century B.C. The inscription says that it was thrown by an athlete called Exoidas, who won a contest with it, then dedicated the discus to Castor and Pollux, the twin sons of Zeus. Pollux was a champion discus thrower.

THE DISCUS THROWER
This famous marble statue of a discus thrower is a copy of a Greek bronze original, perhaps made by the renowned sculptor Myron.

TORCHLIGHT
A runner carrying the Olympic flame at the Seoul Olympics of 1988. In the Athenian games, relay races with torches took place after dark, and the winning team lit a fire on altars to Zeus or Athena.

LONGER JUMPS
Athletes taking part in the long jump used stone or lead jumping weights. This Roman example had grooves so that it could be gripped firmly. Holding the weights, athletes probably threw their arms backward to give themselves extra propulsion on take-off.

BARCELONA GAMES
The 1992 Olympics took place in Barcelona, Spain. The Olympic spirit is still strong today, and cities compete vigorously to host the Games, not only because of their great sporting tradition but also because they bring a great deal of money in trade, commerce, and publicity to the host city.

THE FIRST MODERN OLYMPICS
The first modern Olympics were held in 1896 in Athens. They were organized by Baron Pierre de Coubertin, a Frenchman, who was inspired by the ideals of the ancient Olympic Games.

Wisdom and beauty

FOR THE GREEKS, PHILOSOPHY, or the "love of wisdom," involved not just the way people lived, but a great deal of science as well. Early thinkers were concerned with ideas about the physical world. Heraclitus developed a theory involving atoms, and Pythagoras came up with a geometrical theory as part of his view that the world was based on mathematical patterns. He and his fellow thinkers, both men and women, also believed that souls could be reincarnated – reborn in other bodies – and some even thought that beans might contain the souls of old friends and therefore shouldn't be eaten. Philosophy and the arts were part of religion too. Religious hymns celebrated the meaning of life and explained the origin of the gods. The Greeks made handsome objects both as offerings to the gods and also for their own pleasure and use. Music, sculpture, painting, pottery, and dance all thrived in ancient Greece.

ROYAL PUPIL
Greek philosophers were at the center of Greek life. Here, the philosopher Aristotle is tutoring the young prince Alexander of Macedon (pp. 62–63).

PIPED MUSIC
This pipe from Athens, made out of sycamore wood, is one of a pair; Greeks played sets of double pipes. There was originally a reed in the mouthpiece, so the pipes would have sounded a bit like a modern oboe.

VASE PAINTER
Vase painting is considered to be one of the minor arts, but the work of the potter and painter Exekias was of a very high standard. This exquisitely painted drinking cup shows the god Dionysos reclining in a boat, with his special plant, the vine, twining around the mast. The god, like the vine, was believed to have come from the East. The dolphins may be the pirates who tried to capture him, now turned into sea creatures.

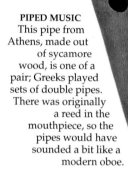

ANIMAL AMPLIFIER
The European tortoise was once plentiful in Greece, and its empty shell made an excellent soundbox for a stringed instrument called the lyre. Its strings, which were plucked with a plectrum (pick), could be tightened to produce a range of notes.

Pythagoras holding the cosmos

THE KEY TO THE COSMOS
Pythagoras (c.580–500 B.C.), originally from the island of Samos, was the leading light of a group of religious thinkers in southern Italy. They believed that the key to the world (cosmos) lay in numbers and mathematical relationships.

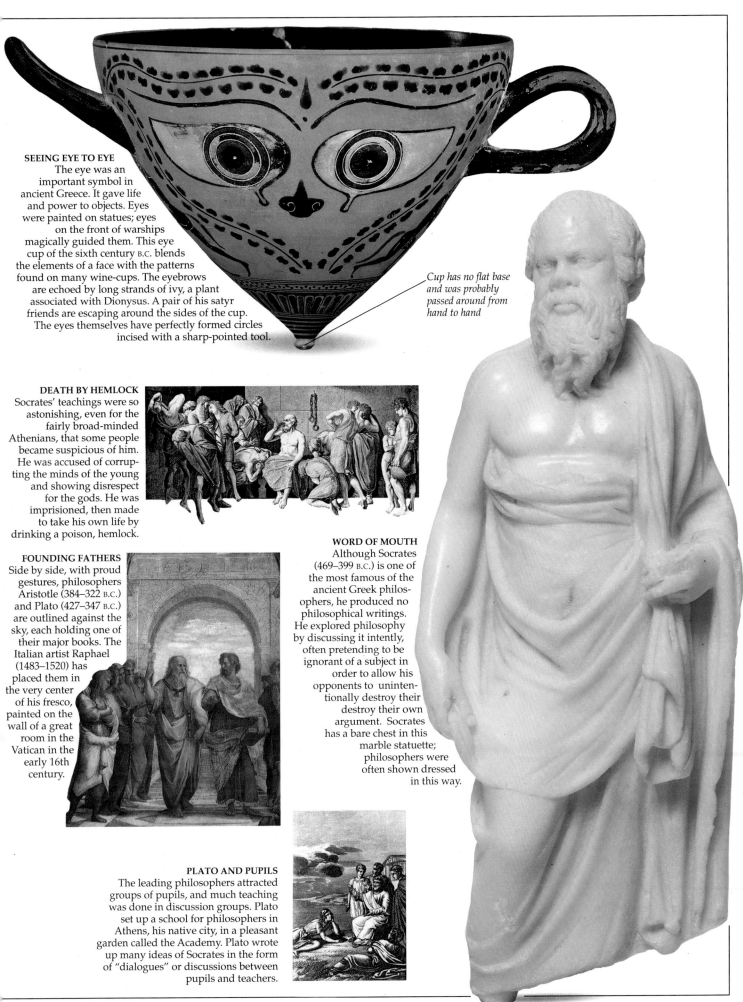

SEEING EYE TO EYE

The eye was an important symbol in ancient Greece. It gave life and power to objects. Eyes were painted on statues; eyes on the front of warships magically guided them. This eye cup of the sixth century B.C. blends the elements of a face with the patterns found on many wine-cups. The eyebrows are echoed by long strands of ivy, a plant associated with Dionysus. A pair of his satyr friends are escaping around the sides of the cup. The eyes themselves have perfectly formed circles incised with a sharp-pointed tool.

Cup has no flat base and was probably passed around from hand to hand

DEATH BY HEMLOCK

Socrates' teachings were so astonishing, even for the fairly broad-minded Athenians, that some people became suspicious of him. He was accused of corrupting the minds of the young and showing disrespect for the gods. He was imprisoned, then made to take his own life by drinking a poison, hemlock.

FOUNDING FATHERS

Side by side, with proud gestures, philosophers Aristotle (384–322 B.C.) and Plato (427–347 B.C.) are outlined against the sky, each holding one of their major books. The Italian artist Raphael (1483–1520) has placed them in the very center of his fresco, painted on the wall of a great room in the Vatican in the early 16th century.

WORD OF MOUTH

Although Socrates (469–399 B.C.) is one of the most famous of the ancient Greek philosophers, he produced no philosophical writings. He explored philosophy by discussing it intently, often pretending to be ignorant of a subject in order to allow his opponents to unintentionally destroy their destroy their own argument. Socrates has a bare chest in this marble statuette; philosophers were often shown dressed in this way.

PLATO AND PUPILS

The leading philosophers attracted groups of pupils, and much teaching was done in discussion groups. Plato set up a school for philosophers in Athens, his native city, in a pleasant garden called the Academy. Plato wrote up many ideas of Socrates in the form of "dialogues" or discussions between pupils and teachers.

Vases and vessels

THE BEST GREEK POTTERY was made in Athens. A high-quality clay was found there, which fired well to a beautiful reddish-brown color. Athenian potters worked in a potters' quarter called the Keramikos, producing huge quantities of wheel-made pottery for use at home and export to other countries. There are various styles of decoration in vase painting. Between 1000 and 700 B.C. geometric patterns were popular. Gradually, around 720 B.C., Oriental motifs came into fashion. The black-figure technique – black silhouette figures painted in a highly refined clay solution on the reddish clay background – was the main way of decorating pots from the early to mid-sixth century B.C. Inner details were cut with a bone or metal tool. Soon after 500 B.C, the red-figure technique took over. The figures of gods and animals were now left in the reddish-brown clay and the background was painted in with a clay solution that, in the firing process, turned black. Many vases in excellent condition have been preserved.

Black-figure amphora

DRINKING UP TIME
Special drinking cups, or *rhytons*, in the form of animal heads were popular. This angry-looking griffin *rhyton* is a good example. The wine would have spilled if the *rhyton* was put down, so perhaps it was passed from person to person until all the wine was gone.

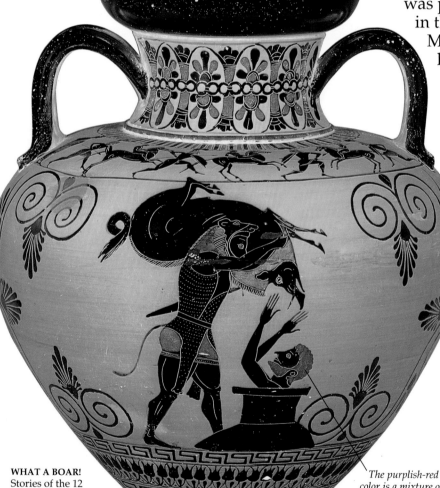

Trefoil top

FIRST SIP
This miniature wine jug is called a *chous*. It shows two schoolboys, one reading from a papyrus scroll and the other holding a lyre. The jug would have been filled with wine and given to a little boy as a special present at the festival of Dionysus, the god of wine.

WHAT A BOAR!
Stories of the 12 labors of Herakles often appeared on vases (pp. 22–23). On this black-figure vase, Herakles holds the Erymanthian boar above King Eurystheus, who cowers in a vase.

The purplish-red color is a mixture of the black clay solution and a red iron oxide

COLLECTOR'S ITEM
This early 19th-century cartoon shows Sir William Hamilton (pp. 42–43), caricatured as a water pot, or *hydria*. Sir William was a great expert on and collector of Greek art, especially vases.

VASE VAULT
In this engraving, Sir William is supervising the opening of an Etruscan tomb in Italy. The skeleton is surrounded by vases that were exported from Athens.

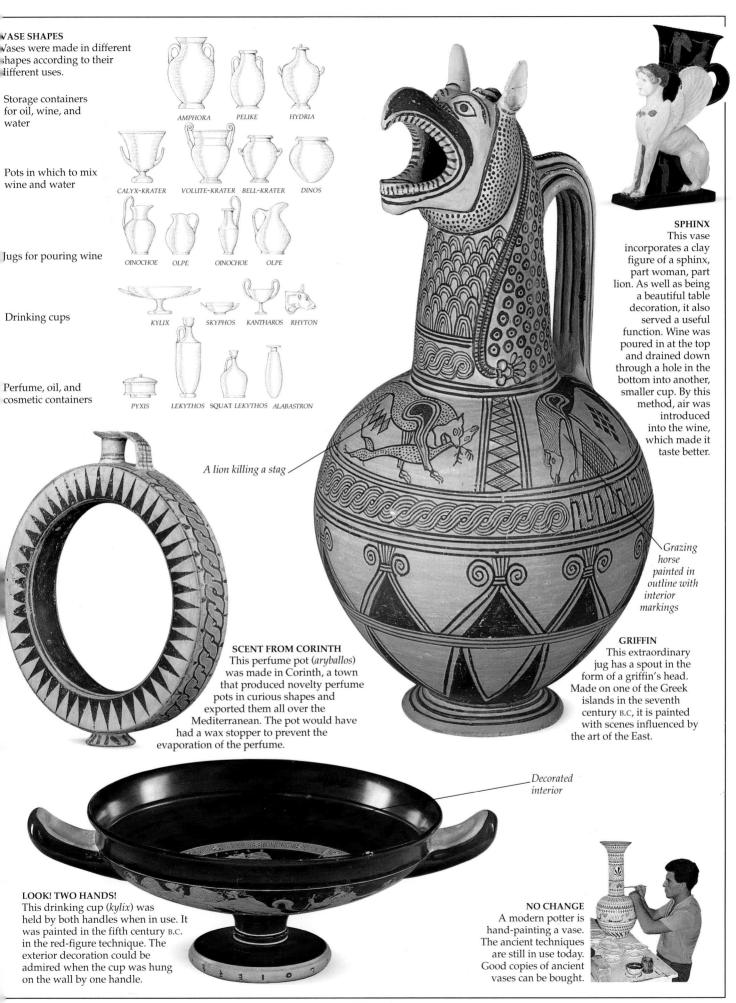

VASE SHAPES
Vases were made in different shapes according to their different uses.

Storage containers for oil, wine, and water

AMPHORA PELIKE HYDRIA

Pots in which to mix wine and water

CALYX-KRATER VOLUTE-KRATER BELL-KRATER DINOS

Jugs for pouring wine

OINOCHOE OLPE OINOCHOE OLPE

Drinking cups

KYLIX SKYPHOS KANTHAROS RHYTON

Perfume, oil, and cosmetic containers

PYXIS LEKYTHOS SQUAT LEKYTHOS ALABASTRON

A lion killing a stag

SPHINX
This vase incorporates a clay figure of a sphinx, part woman, part lion. As well as being a beautiful table decoration, it also served a useful function. Wine was poured in at the top and drained down through a hole in the bottom into another, smaller cup. By this method, air was introduced into the wine, which made it taste better.

Grazing horse painted in outline with interior markings

SCENT FROM CORINTH
This perfume pot (*aryballos*) was made in Corinth, a town that produced novelty perfume pots in curious shapes and exported them all over the Mediterranean. The pot would have had a wax stopper to prevent the evaporation of the perfume.

GRIFFIN
This extraordinary jug has a spout in the form of a griffin's head. Made on one of the Greek islands in the seventh century B.C, it is painted with scenes influenced by the art of the East.

Decorated interior

LOOK! TWO HANDS!
This drinking cup (*kylix*) was held by both handles when in use. It was painted in the fifth century B.C. in the red-figure technique. The exterior decoration could be admired when the cup was hung on the wall by one handle.

NO CHANGE
A modern potter is hand-painting a vase. The ancient techniques are still in use today. Good copies of ancient vases can be bought.

Farming, fishing, and food

Life on a greek farm was difficult, as the soil in much of Greece is of poor quality. Greek farmers plowed in spring and then again in autumn. Plows, which were pulled by oxen, were made of wood and sometimes tipped with iron to make them sharper. The farm worker followed the plow, scattering seed such as barley, by hand. Farmers prayed to Zeus and Demeter, the goddess of the grain, for a good harvest. On the slopes of the hills were vineyards and picked grapes drying in the sun. Other grapes were gathered to make wine, the most popular Greek drink. Most towns and villages were near the sea, and a variety of fish was caught using bronze fishhooks. Wealthy people hunted wild deer, boar, and hare. Poorer people ate meat only on special festival occasions when animals were sacrificed to the gods and then shared among the worshipers.

DINNER SERVICE
Wealthy people always ate while reclining on a couch. Slaves would bring in food and place it on a small table in front of the diner. This bronze banqueter is said to have come from Dodona in northwestern Greece.

TIME STANDS STILL
This shepherd and flock going home for the night look the same as they would have in ancient times.

HUNTING AND FISHING
This fresco of a Bronze Age fisherman came from Santorini, a volcanic island near Crete. Perhaps he was bringing the fish to the palace there as an offering. The hunter is carrying a fox and a hare; his hunting dog runs beside him. He would not have eaten the fox, but might have made a warm hat from the fur.

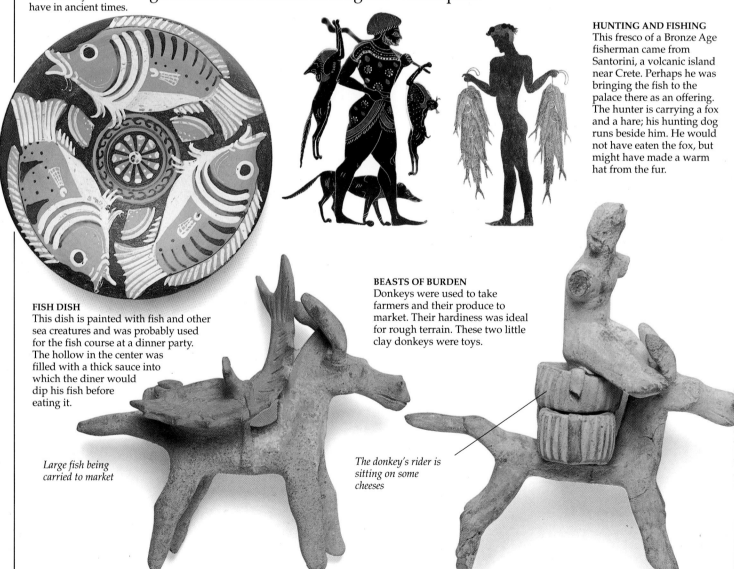

FISH DISH
This dish is painted with fish and other sea creatures and was probably used for the fish course at a dinner party. The hollow in the center was filled with a thick sauce into which the diner would dip his fish before eating it.

BEASTS OF BURDEN
Donkeys were used to take farmers and their produce to market. Their hardiness was ideal for rough terrain. These two little clay donkeys were toys.

Large fish being carried to market

The donkey's rider is sitting on some cheeses

Duck's head decorates the end of the strainer

SWIMMING IN OIL
This little dolphin skimming over the waves is an oil container, used in food preparation. Dolphins were common in the waters off Greece.

FINE WINE
Wine, the most popular Greek drink, was enjoyed at all times of the day. It was thick, needed straining, and was nearly always diluted with water. This wine strainer is made of bronze. Many different utensils and containers were used for the storing, serving, and drinking of wine.

ATTIC OIL
Attica, the region around Athens, was famous for its olive groves. Olive oil was used in cooking, washing, and oil lamps.

OLIVE HARVEST
Olive trees grow abundantly in Greece. On this vase, four people are gathering olives. One is sitting up in the tree, two are shaking the branches with sticks, and on the ground below, another is gathering the fallen olives in a basket.

Dregs collected in the bottom of the strainer

Fossilized snail on egg

GOAT FOR ALL SEASONS
Goats were useful animals. They required only rough grazing ground and provided milk, cheese and warm clothing for country people in winter. This little bronze goat was made about 500 B.C.

EGG CUP
Five hen's eggs in a terra-cotta cup were found in a tomb on the island of Rhodes. They are over 2,000 years old. Many households kept hens, and eggs were an important part of the daily diet. Funeral offerings of eggs, both real like these or stone or clay imitations, were common in Greek graves. They seem to have been symbols of life after death.

Crafts, travel, and trade

STONE CARVERS, METAL WORKERS, jewelers, shoemakers, and many other craftspeople flourished in the cities of Greece. Their workshops were usually in the center of town around the *agora*, or marketplace. People would come to buy their products, and farmers from the countryside would sell vegetables, fruit, and cheese. There were also weights-and-measures officials, money-changers, acrobats, dancers, and slaves standing on platforms waiting to be sold. Most ordinary people did not travel far from home (except to war), because there were few good roads. The faithful donkey was the most reliable form of transport for shorter journeys. If a Greek wanted to travel a long distance, he would usually go by boat around the coast, thereby avoiding the mountains that cover much of the country. There was a great deal of trade between the city-states and the Greek colonies, as well as with other Mediterranean countries. Oil, wine, pottery, and metal work were the main exports.

FISHY BUSINESS
Fishing provides a livelihood for many Greeks today, just as it did in ancient times. A modern fisherman on the island of Mykonos is mending his nets.

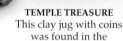

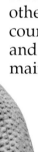

TEMPLE TREASURE
This clay jug with coins was found in the foundations of the temple of Artemis at Ephesus. The coins, made of electrum, probably date from 650–625 B.C. This was soon after coinage was introduced into Greece from Lydia in Asia Minor (roughly, modern Turkey), where coins were invented.

Coin showing the infant Herakles strangling snakes

THREE COINS
As a symbol of independence, each city-state issued its own coins, which were at first made of electrum (an alloy of gold and silver) and later solely of silver or occasionally gold. They were often beautifully decorated with the symbols of Greek deities, and many modern coins have been modeled on them.

Coin showing Cyrus, the king of Persia

A tortoise coin from the island of Aegina

INTO AFRICA
This pot in the form of the head of an African is evidence of the widespread trading contacts of the Greeks. They were not, however, very adventurous sailors, preferring to keep the coast in sight when on long voyages.

BEASTS OF BURDEN
Donkeys could carry heavy burdens and negotiate narrow mountain tracks. They still do today.

COBBLER
This cobbler is depicted at the bottom of a red figure cup. He is bending over strips of leather that he is cutting and shaping. Boots, sandals, and tools hang from the wall above him. This scene would have become visible to the drinker when he had drained his cup.

AT THE LOOM
Upright looms, just like this one in use today, were used by women in Classical times to make woolen clothing, drapes, and furniture fabrics. Weaving was regarded as a noble as well as a necessary task.

BLACKSMITH
This painting on a jug shows a blacksmith at work. His furnace is a brick-built shaft fueled with charcoal. Bellows would have been used to fan the flames. The metal, which was placed inside the shaft, trickled down to form a lump at the bottom, which the blacksmith can here be seen removing with a pair of tongs.

POTTER
The Greeks are famous for their beautiful pottery. Every town had its potters' quarter (pp. 48–49) where pots were made and sold. On this wine cup, a potter sits at his wheel, the speed of which he controls with his knee. Above him on a shelf are some of his pots, and below him (now slightly damaged) sits a pet dog who is watching his master at work.

DEEP-SEA FISHING
A great variety of fish were available in the deeper waters. Wooden vessels, like this modern one, were used for such fishing expeditions. Eel and salted fish were favorite Greek delicacies.

Warfare

SHIELDED
This Greek vase painting shows how the soldier wore his shield, passing his arm under an iron bar and gripping a leather strap at the rim.

WARFARE WAS a normal part of Greek life, and the city-states frequently fought one another. Many Greek men, therefore, had to join an army, and from the earliest times had to pay for their own armor and equipment. In Athens, boys trained as soldiers between age 18 and 20, after which they could be called up for military service. In Sparta training began much earlier (pp. 56–57). Athenian soldiers were led by ten commanders called *strategoi*. The infantry (foot soldiers) were the backbone of the Greek armies; they fought in close formations called phalanxes. Poorer soldiers served in auxiliary units as archers and stoneslingers. When laying siege to cities, the armies of Hellenistic Greece used catapults, flame throwers, battering rams, and cauldrons of burning coals and sulfur. Athens controlled its empire by means of oar-powered warships, or triremes. At the height of its power, it had about 300 triremes.

BATTLE OF SALAMIS
The famous sea battle of Salamis was a turning point in the Persian wars (pp. 18–19). It took place just off the coast of Athens in 480 B.C. and was a triumphant victory for the Greeks over the Persian fleet. As a result of this battle, the Persian king Xerxes and much of his army went back to Asia, abandoning the invasion of Greece.

SPEEDY BEASTS
Greek chariots were often decorated with animals associated with speed. These bronze horses were once attached to a fast chariot.

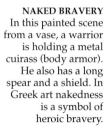

NAKED BRAVERY
In this painted scene from a vase, a warrior is holding a metal cuirass (body armor). He also has a long spear and a shield. In Greek art nakedness is a symbol of heroic bravery.

Helmet with nose protection

Body armor

HOPLITE
Greek soldiers were called hoplites, from the word *hoplon*, meaning shield. Only men from wealthy families could be hoplites, because only they could afford expensive armor and weapons.

Greaves

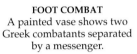

FOOT COMBAT
A painted vase shows two
Greek combatants separated
by a messenger.

HELMETS
Helmets protected the
head from every sort
of slash and from
blows and knocks.
They varied in shape,
and some had crests
made of horsehair to
make the wearer
appear more impressive
and frightening.

Attic helmet has
no nose guard

Corinthian helmet
with long nosepiece
and cheek guards

BREASTPLATE
The cuirass (breastplate or body armor)
was usually made of bronze. It
protected all the upper body parts.
Cuirasses were made to measure,
each man being specially fitted.
More expensive cuirasses had
ridges, roughly aligned to the body
muscles, which were meant to
deflect blows. The cuirass was
made of two plates joined at the
sides by leather straps. The side areas,
therefore, were the most vulnerable
parts of the body.

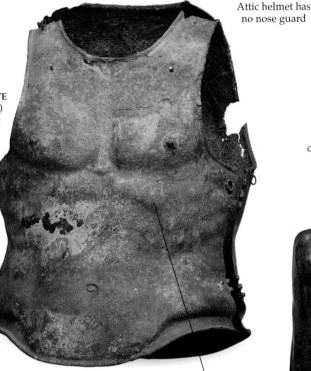

*Sculpted ridges
roughly
aligning with
chest muscles*

GREAVES
Hoplites wore bronze leg guards
called greaves (below) to protect the
lower part of their legs in battle.
Some of these greaves may have
originally been fixed onto large
statues of heroic warriors in
southern Italy.

WARSHIP
The fastest Greek ship was called a trireme; 170 oarsmen were needed to row it. They sat in
three levels, one above the other, on either side of the boat. At the prow was a pointed ram
strengthened with metal, which could sink enemy ships. There was often an eye painted on
the prow (pp. 46–47). This illustration shows two sails, but warships may have had only
one, probably made of linen and lowered when the ship was engaged in battle.

*The long spear
was the main
weapon of the
Greek infantry*

CHAMPION FIGHT
This red-figure vase shows a fight between
two heroes of the Trojan War, Achilles and
Hector (pp. 12–13). The vase painter has
clearly painted the blood flowing from the
wound just above Hector's knee. Both
heroes are wearing the helmets and armor
worn by soldiers of the 5th century B.C.

The state of Sparta

S PARTA, IN SOUTHERN GREECE, WAS FOUNDED in the tenth century B.C. by the Dorians, who defeated the original inhabitants of the area. Two centuries later, Sparta conquered its neighbor, Messenia, and gained excellent agricultural land. It became a luxury-loving state producing fine crafts. Music and poetry also flourished. Later the Spartans were defeated in war, and the conquered Messenians engaged in a long-running rebellion, so Sparta turned to military matters. It became a superpower in Greece and the main rival of Athens, and Spartan society was dominated by the need to maintain power. All men of Spartan birth had to serve in the army. Their whole lives were dedicated to learning the arts of war. Boys of seven were taken from their families to live in army barracks. Non-citizens in Sparta were either *perioikoi* or *helots*. The *perioikoi* were free men who, although they did not have the rights of citizens, were allowed to trade and serve in the army. *Helots* were the descendants of the original inhabitants of the area. They farmed the land and did the heavy work for their Spartan overlords.

HARBOR BATTLE
The Piraeus is the port of Athens, 4 miles (6 km) to the southwest of the city. In this engraving it is being besieged by Spartan ships in 388 B.C.

NATURAL PROTECTION
This 19th-century German engraving shows the site of Sparta in a fertile plain of Lakonia in southern Greece. Its remoteness was an advantage to the warring Spartans, and the high mountains to the east, north, and west, and the sea to the south, formed natural defenses.

SPARTAN WARRIOR
The Greek historian Herodotus wrote that Spartan soldiers, like this one of the fifth century B.C., always combed their long hair when they felt they might be about to put their lives at risk, as when going into battle. The scarlet color of the military cloaks became a symbol of Spartan pride.

THE YOUNG SPARTANS
Spartan scenes were a popular subject with artists of the 19th century. This unusual painting by the French Impressionist painter Edgar Degas (1834–1917) shows boys and girls exercising in the valley of the Eurotas River, which runs through Sparta. The girls look much more aggressive than girls from other Greek cities.

SPARTAN REGIME
The Spartan system of education, with its emphasis on physical fitness, was much admired in 19th-century England. Corporal (physical) punishment too was regarded as character-forming for schoolboys, just as it was in ancient Sparta. The violence in this cartoon by British cartoonist George Cruikshank (1792–1878) suggests that he thought otherwise.

OFFERINGS
Thousands of small figurines have been found at a sanctuary of Artemis Orthia on the banks of the Eurotas River at Sparta. Among animals such as stags, dogs, and horses are representations of Artemis herself. There are also figurines of the goddess Athena wearing a helmet. The figurines were made at the sanctuary and sold to visitors, who often left them behind as offerings to the goddess. It was to this sanctuary that Spartan boys were taken to be whipped as a demonstration of their toughness and endurance.

Artemis

Warrior

Artemis

Figure playing pipes

A stag

IN THE LEAD
This girl is taking part in a running race and is looking back to see how far she is in the lead. She is wearing a very short skirt, which no girl from any other Greek city would dare to wear. Girls did not fight in wars but, like most boys, they were trained in running and for an outdoor life. This made them fit and strong so that they would have healthy babies who would grow up to be good soldiers.

Science and medicine

THE GREEKS WERE INTERESTED in science and, influenced by Egyptian and Babylonian scholars, made advances in biology, mathematics, astronomy, and geography. In the third century B.C., the astronomer, Aristarchus, already understood that the earth revolved around the sun, and another astronomer, Anaxagoras (500–428 B.C.), discovered that the moon reflected sunlight. The most advanced scientific work took place in Hellenistic times (pp. 62–63). An important area of Greek science was medicine. The Greeks believed that illness was a punishment sent by the gods to whom they prayed for a cure. Sanctuaries of the god Asclepius (the god of medicine) were found all over the Greek world. The most famous one was at Epidaurus. Many sick people came there and spent the night in the temple. They believed that Asclepius appeared to them in "dreams" to prescribe treatments such as herbal remedies, diets, and exercises. The next day, the priests would carry out the treatment and many people went away cured. The Greeks developed sophisticated medical treatments for all kinds of diseases. These treatments, based on practical research, grew out of the Asclepiad cult and were practised by Hippocrates (460–377 B.C.) who is often described as the founder of modern medicine.

ASCLEPIADES
Asclepiades was a famous Greek doctor of the first century B.C. He was very knowledgeable in the theory and practice of medicine, but he also believed in wine as an aid to recovery and the importance of a pleasant bedside manner, so he was very popular with all his patients.

IT ALL ADDS UP
This engraving from a philosophy book of the 1400s shows the Roman philosopher Boethius (A.D. 480–524) doing mathematical calculations, and the Greek mathematician Pythagoras (pp. 46–47) working at an abacus. The woman in the centre is probably a muse of learning.

TEMPLE OF ASCLEPIUS
In this engraving, people can be seen approaching a statue of the god Asclepius. He is sitting on a throne and holding his staff which has a serpent twisted round it. A real snake, regarded as sacred and kept in all temples to Asclepius, can be seen slithering along the plinth.

ABACUS
The Greeks used a counting frame called an abacus for mathematical calculations. It had beads threaded in lines on wires. Some lines had beads which counted as 1, others had the value of 10 and others, 100. By moving the beads around, complicated multiplication and division could be achieved.

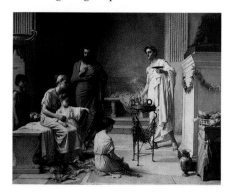

TEMPLE VISIT
In this painting by the 19th-century artist John William Waterhouse (1849–1917) a child has been brought by his mother to the temple of Asclepius. Priests stand around waiting to interpret the god's wishes.

THANKS

Patients who had been cured by Asclepius often left a model of the part of their body affected by illness, as an offering of thanks to the god for curing them. This marble relief of a leg has an inscription to Asclepius carved upon it and was dedicated by a worshipper called Tyche.

ΑϹΚΛΗ
ΠΙΩ
ΚΑΙ
ΫΓΕΙΑ
ΤΥΧΗ
ΕΥΧΑΡΙϹ
ΤΗΡΙΟΝ

HIPPOCRATES

The famous physician, Hippocrates, was born on the island of Kos. He wrote 53 scientific books on medical topics, now known as the *Corpus*. He taught that the human body was a single organism and each part could only be understood in the context of the whole. Modern doctors still take the Hippocratic Oath which is the basis of medical ethics.

MODERN MODELS

The practice of leaving a model of the affected part of the body as a thanks offering, still continues in churches in some countries today. These modern examples are from Athens.

TOKENS

These modern silver tokens are also thanks for cures. The animals indicate that people believed that they too could be cured with the help of offerings.

Death and the afterlife

KING OF THE UNDERWORLD
Zeus ruled the earth and sky;
Poseidon, the sea. The third of
these divine brothers was Hades,
king of the underworld, also
known as Pluto. Eventually the
underworld came to be known
simply as Hades.

DEATH CAME EARLY for most people in
ancient times, because life was very
harsh. Young men often died in battle;
young women died in childbirth. The
Greeks believed in – or hoped for –
some kind of life after death, although
their ideas about this state varied. The
kingdom of the dead was generally
thought to be deep in the earth, and
therefore many people buried their
dead. But sometimes corpses were
cremated on a funeral pyre. The soul was sometimes shown as a tiny
winged person, and some Greeks believed that it escaped from the body
and rose up to become one of the stars, waiting until it could be reborn
in a new body. Gods such as Dionysus, who, like the vines he protected,
died and was reborn each year, gave people hope of new life. The corn
goddess, Demeter, whose daughter, Persephone, was snatched away by
Hades, the god of the underworld, claimed back her daughter for part
of the year (spring and summer). Tombs were decorated with pictures
of feasts and the dead person's favorite things, and food was placed in
the grave, so that the dead could be happy in the afterlife.

THE DIVER
This delightful painting was found on the
inside of a stone sarcophagus (coffin) found at
Poseidonia, a Greek city in southern Italy,
later called Paestum. It probably represents
the leap of the dead into the unknown.

FLASK OF FAREWELL
Offerings to the dead included
narrow flasks known as *lekythoi*,
which contained oil used to anoint
the body. They were decorated
with delicately painted scenes of
farewell. This dead warrior,
perhaps a victim of one of the
many wars in fifth-century B.C.
Greece, receives his helmet from a
woman. The goose at their feet,
the bird of Aphrodite (pp. 20–21),
hints at their relationship.

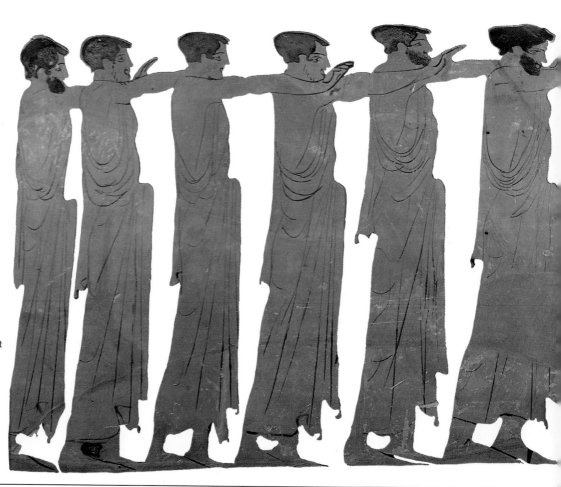

FARE FOR THE FERRYMAN

Charon was the grim ferryman who carried people across the black waters of the river Styx and into the kingdom of the dead. In this painting by John Stanhope (pp. 12–13), the underworld is a gloomy place with whispering reeds and spindly trees through which dead souls can be seen making their way to the river. The one-way trip in Charon's punt cost one Greek coin. The family of the dead sometimes left a coin on the corpse for the journey.

THE ENTRANCE TO HADES

Ancient people thought that certain places might be the entrance to the underworld. Many Greeks settled near Solfatara in southern Italy, where the steaming sulfur lake made it a prime candidate.

DEATH BEFORE DISHONOR

After the death of Achilles, the great warrior Ajax failed to become the champion of the Greeks fighting at Troy. He could not live with the shame, so he killed himself by falling on his sword. This famous incident from the Trojan War is often shown on painted pots and is also the subject of a play by Sophocles (pp. 38–39).

TOMBSTONE

At certain periods in Athens, tombstones, carved in marble and originally painted in bright colors, were placed above graves. Above the carving of the dead person, the sloping lines of a roof suggested a temple or shrine. Here the dead man, Xanthippos, sits on an elegant curved chair, his children shown on a smaller scale beside him. His name is carved above him. It is not really known why he was holding a foot; possibly he was a shoemaker.

MOURNING LINE

A Greek funeral was a dramatic event. The body was laid out on a couch, with the feet facing the door to ensure that the spirit would leave. A wreath was placed on the head. A procession of mourners wearing black robes escorted the corpse. The women cut off their long hair as a sign of grief and gave a lock of it to the dead person. They also tore at their cheeks until the blood ran.

Alexander and the Hellenistic age

EXCAVATION AT EPHESUS
Ephesus was a teeming city on the coast of Asia Minor where Greeks and people of many other nationalities lived together. The city and its famous sanctuary, dedicated to the goddess Artemis, thrived in the Hellenistic period and throughout the Roman era.

IN THE FOURTH CENTURY B.C., a strong king called Philip II turned Macedonia, in the north, into the most powerful state in Greece. After his assassination in 336 B.C., his 20-year-old son Alexander, a military genius, took over the reins of power. Not content with ruling Greece, he invaded Persian territory in 334 B.C. and then pressed on through Asia Minor, then south and east to Egypt, Afghanistan, and India. He established new Greek cities, such as Alexandria in Egypt, and thus spread Greek culture over a vast area. Alexander, called the Great, intended to create a huge empire, incorporating most of the then known world. His death of a fever in 323 B.C. ended this ambition, and his vast empire was divided among his quarreling generals. The period from the death of Alexander until about 30 B.C. is known as the Hellenistic Age, from the word "Hellene," meaning Greek. The Hellenistic kingdoms preserved many aspects of Greek life but were eventually overcome by the rising power of Rome.

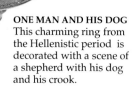

Ruins at Pergamum

ONE MAN AND HIS DOG
This charming ring from the Hellenistic period is decorated with a scene of a shepherd with his dog and his crook.

APHRODITE
Terra-cotta figurines of Aphrodite, goddess of love and beauty, were popular in Hellenistic times. She is nearly always shown without any clothes, sometimes tying a ribbon in her hair, sometimes bending down to fasten her sandal.

Ruins at Pergamum

TOWN PLANNING
Pergamum, a Hellenistic city in Asia Minor, was the power base of the wealthy Attalid dynasty. The ruins of temples and other opulent civic buildings can still be seen on the terraces cut into the steep mountain site. The people of Pergamum must have enjoyed spectacular views over the surrounding countryside.

EROS DIADEM
Alexander's troops captured a great deal of Persian gold, and gold jewelery became very fashionable in aristocratic circles. Elaborate diadems, closely resembling crowns, have been found. Fixed at the front of this spectacular diadem is a tiny figure of Eros, the personification of love, holding a jug.

ALEXANDER'S EMPIRE

Alexander did not just want to build an empire, he also wanted it to last. To stop rebellion and invasion by conquered peoples, he founded many colonies populated by his own former soldiers who followed the Greek way of life. On the whole he treated the conquered peoples with respect and encouraged his men to marry Eastern women. His conquests came to an end in India because his men refused to fight any farther.

Richard Burton in the 1956 film *Alexander the Great*

TRUNK CHARGER

This coin shows Alexander on horseback attacking two Indian warriors mounted on an elephant. It is thought to have been issued in Babylon in 323 B.C.

WALL OF FIRE

In 327 B.C., Alexander crossed the Himalayan Mountains intending to conquer India. But a terrible battle forced him to turn back to Babylon. Alexander's fame lived on in legend. This Indian painting, painted over 1,000 years after his time, shows him building a defensive wall of fire.

THE DEFEAT OF DARIUS

Alexander finally defeated the Persian king Darius III in 331 B.C. in a long and bloody battle at Gaugamela in Mesopotamia (southwest Asia). Darius fled, and afterward Alexander called himself King of Asia. In this etching, he can be seen on horseback, fighting fearlessly.

FAMILY OF DARIUS

In this painting by the Italian artist Paolo Veronese (1528–1588), Alexander is shown receiving the submission of the family of his defeated enemy Darius. Notice that the artist has portrayed everyone in 16th-century clothes.

Index

Acknowledgments

Dorling Kindersley would like to thank:

The Department of Greek and Roman Antiquities, the British Museum for providing ancient artefacts for photography. Patsy Vanags of the British Museum Education Service for her assistance with the text. Bill Gordon for his superb model of a Greek farmhouse on pp. 28-29. Alan Meek for the armour and weapons on pp. 54-55. Helena Spiteri, Andrew Chiakli and Toby Williams for modelling the clothes and armor. Anita Burger for hairdressing and make-up. Gin Van Noorden and Helena Spiteri for editorial assistance. Earl Neish and Manisha Patel for design assistance. Jane Parker for the index.

Picture credits
t=top, b=bottom, c=centre, l=left, r=right

Front cover: Head of Aphrodite, British Museum, Michael Holford.

Allsport: Gray Mortimore 45cl; Vandystadt 45c.
American School of Classical Studies, Athens: 32tlb.
Ancient Art & Architecture Collection: 12tr, 44tl, 56cl, 63cr.
Ashmolean Museum, Oxford: 9tl.
Bildarchiv Preussicher Kulturbestitz (Antikenmuseum Berlin) 33tr.
Bridgeman Art Library: 13tl De Morgan Foundation; 18br Palace of Westminster; 20tl House of Masks, Delos; 30tl Private Collection; 42b Private Collection; 46c Staatliche Antikensammlungen, Munchen; 47b Vatican Museums; 50cr Museo Nationale, Athens; 56cb.
National Gallery, London; 58br Fine Art

Society; 60tl; 61tl.
Trustees of the British Museum: 16tr, 16bl, 16br, 17c, 17bc, 17br, 18tr, 19c, 19b, 20bl, 40tl, 47tr, 47br, 48bc; 48br
c Dr John Coates: 55cb.
Photo DAI Athen: 12c (neg. Mykonos 70).
Ekdotike Athenon: 52bl.
ET Archive: 62cr.
Mary Evans Picture Library: 18tl, 26cl, 31cl, 35cr, 38tr, 39tl, 44b, 46tr, 46br, 47c, 47bc, 54c, 56tl, 56c, 56bl, 58tl, 58c, 58cr, 59, 63cb.Sonia Halliday: 8tl, 11tc, 11tr, 12bl, 20tr, 25tl, 25tr, 25c, 33c, 44cr.
Robert Harding Picture Library: /G. White 16c; 38c, 49br, 52bc, 53cl, 59bl.
Michael Holford: 6tr, 7tr, 9bl, 16tl, 20br, 21c. Hulton Picture Co: 45b..
Image Bank: 51c, 52tl, 53br, 59bc.
Kobal Collection: 63c..
Mansell Collection: 11tl, 12tl, 12tc, 62tl.
The National Gallery, London: 9cr.
SPADEM; 12br, 21tr, 22tr, 23bl, 63b.
Anne Pearson: 24br.

Photostage /c Donald Cooper: 39tc.
Royal Ontario Museum: 17tl.
Scala: 8b Heraklion Museum; 11bc, 20cl.
Museo Nationale, Athens; 24bl Delphi Museum; 26b; 35tl The Vatican Museums; 36tl, 38b, 41b; 44cl MNA; 58cl Museo del Terme.
Zefa: Konrad Helbig 17tc; K. Scholz 19tr; Damm 25cl;Konrad Helbig 26tl; Starfoto 50tl; 62c.

Every effort has been made to trace the copyright-holders. Dorling Kindersley apologises for any unintentional omissions and would be pleased, in such cases, to add an acknowledgement in future editions.

Illustrations by: John Woodcock and John Hutchinson.

Maps by: Sallie Alane Reason

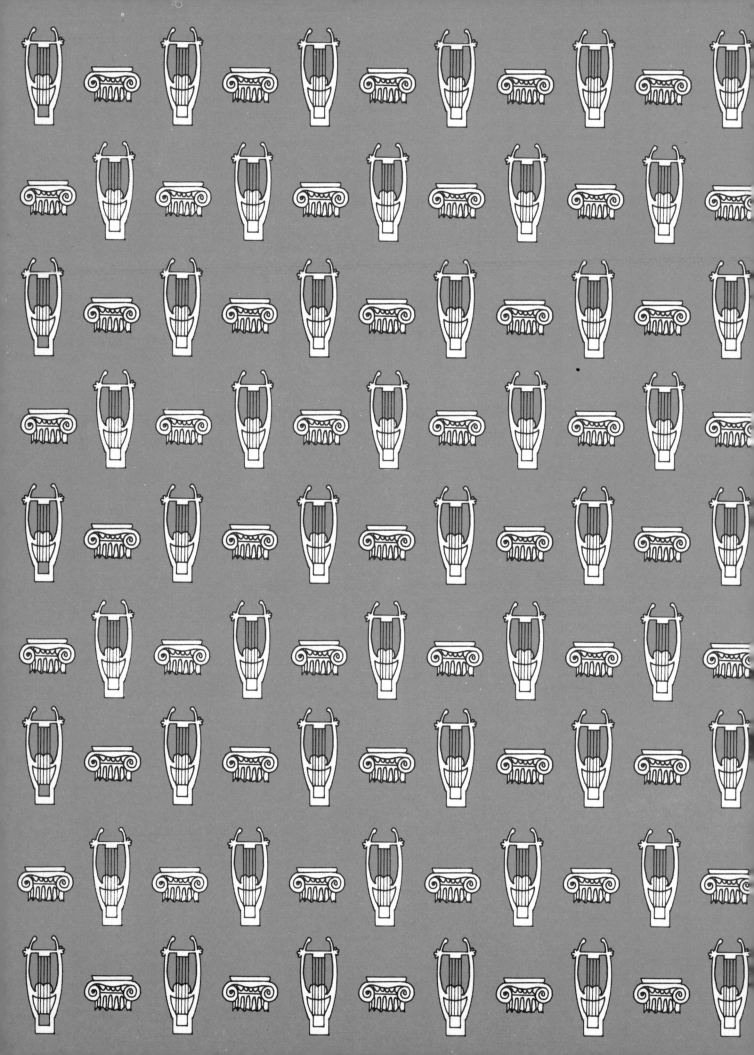